The Value of Complete Rest

Finding Rest in a Restless Age

BOOK 1

Copyright © 2018 C. Richard McCaw
All rights reserved.
No part of this publication may be reproduced,
stored in a retrieval system, or transmitted in any form
or by any means, electronic, photocopying, recording or scanning,
except for brief quotations in critical reviews or articles
without the written permission of the author.

Unless otherwise indicated,
most biblical quotations are taken
from the New King James Version®.
Copyright © 1982 by Thomas Nelson. Used by permission.
All rights reserved.

Scripture quotations are also taken
from the Amplified® Bible Classic Edition (AMPC),
Copyright © 1954, 1958, 1962, 1964, 1965, 1987
by The Lockman Foundation
Used by permission. www.Lockman.org.

Paraphrased passages are indicated.

ISBN-13:978-1720673484

ISBN-10:1720673489

The VALUE of Complete REST - BOOK 1 Finding REST in a Restless Age

MOST HIGH DEDICATION

This book is dedicated to the Lord Jesus Christ,
the Exalted, Risen Son of God

**Blessing and honor and glory and power
be to Him Who sits on the throne,
and to the Lamb,
forever and ever
(Rev 5:13)**

The VALUE of Complete REST - BOOK 1 Finding REST in a Restless Age

Table of Contents

Introduction	vii
Foreword	xiii
Preface	xvii
Acknowledgements	xx
Chapter 1. Our Desperate Need for Rest	1
Chapter 2. Rest for the Weary	5
Chapter 3. Our Instinctive Need for Love	7
Chapter 4. Our Instinctive Need for Worship	13
Chapter 5. The Danger of Ignorance	17
Chapter 6. The Consequences of Ignorance	23
Chapter 7. The Danger of Unbiblical Traditions	27
Chapter 8. Spiritual Death-Traps	31
Chapter 9. Out Instinctive Need for Law	35
Chapter 10. The Fruit of Lawlessness	37
Chapter 11. Divine Orders	39
Chapter 12. Cycles of Rest	45
Chapter 13. Defining the Lord's Day	51
Chapter 14. Accept no Substitute!	57
Chapter 15. Father knows Best	61
Chapter 16. The Supreme Example	65
Chapter 17. An Old Commandment	69

QUESTIONS AND ANSWERS

- The Need for Rest	73
- The Appointed Day	83

CONCLUSION 93

About the Author 95

The VALUE of Complete REST - BOOK 1 Finding REST in a Restless Age

INTRODUCTION

*T*his book has been designed for the believer who loves the Lord Jesus Christ with the whole heart, soul, mind and strength. It attempts to shed much light upon a very difficult subject. This presents an enormous challenge, since the Body of Christ, known as the Church, has been cut off from its Hebrew roots for centuries.

Imagine someone whose index finger has been sliced off while doing carpentry. The presiding doctor will have to be very skilled, accurate and patient as he operates.

The individual who sincerely wants to discover God's will on this subject will be searching the scriptures, and not swallowing wholesale perspectives presented anywhere, not even those in this book.

A man, who prospects for gold, will dig hard and deep and will come across stones that seem like gold, but will carefully examine each one to determine their authenticity. He may have to throw away many pieces, but in the end he will discover that the genuine article sparkles in the sun.

As committed believers we must study the scriptures with an open mind and an open heart. If we search the scriptures diligently, we will discover what the Bible really teaches (Acts 17:11).

How the reader should use this book

Careful attention must also be paid to the historical and Jewish context, not forgetting that the Bible was written at a specific time and place, and given to a particular people.

As you begin this study, therefore, remember that the human heart is *"deceitful above all things, and it is exceedingly perverse and corrupt and severely, mortally sick! Who can know it [perceive, understand, be acquainted with his own heart and mind]?"* (Jer 17:9 AMPC).

Isaiah, the prophet, long ago wrote, *"All we like sheep have gone astray; we have turned everyone to his own way," (Isa 53:6) and "all our righteousness (our best deeds of rightness and justice) is like filthy rags or a polluted garment!"* (Isa 64:6 AMPC).

Even if we are religious, deep in the human heart, subconscious evil motives often drive us to pursue our own goals and imaginations. Filled with our own ways, we become bent on departing from God. **"My thoughts are not your thoughts, neither are your ways My ways,"** says the Lord. **"For as the heavens are higher than the earth, so are My ways higher than your ways and My thoughts than your thoughts"** (Isa 55:8).

The Pharisees of Jesus' time were deeply religious and knew all the right words and phrases. They were very protective of religious traditions, having spent years following Moses, the prophets and famous teachers. Nevertheless, Jesus told them, **"Search and investigate and pore over the Scriptures diligently, because you suppose and trust that you have eternal life through them"** (John 5:39 AMPC). They were very strict, unmerciful and judgmental, even twisting the meaning of the law to allow them to steal the property of widows and orphans in the name of God.

If we understand that religion is man's effort without God to do good works, then we can see why such efforts are bound to fail. Jesus told them, **"I know you and recognize and understand**

that you have not the love of God in you" (John 5:42 AMPC).

They were blind to the sinfulness of their own hearts and totheir deep need of a deliverer. Although Jesus Christ, stood daily before them, they continually rejected Him as God's provision for achieving righteousness through faith.

"I have come in My Father's name and with His power," Jesus told them, **"and you do not receive Me [your hearts are not open to Me, you give Me no welcome]!"** (John 5; 43 AMPC).

Jesus very gently outlined for us the steps to spiritual revelation that will unravel the issue of the Sabbath or any other controversial spiritual issue.

1. With a child-like spirit, we must abandon preconceived ideas and diligently dig deep into God's Word in order to see Christ in every scripture. Jesus informed the Pharisees, **"These [very Scriptures] testify about Me!"** (John 5:39 AMPC)

2. Loving God must be more than *saying "I love you, Lord!"* In the community of believers in which He has placed us, we must work together to establish His kingdom on earth (Acts 1:8). Our love must move beyond mere words and translate into action.

3. Pure faith must flow out of an intimate relationship with God. Jesus therefore challenged the Pharisees, **"How is it possible for you to believe [how can you learn to believe], you who [are content to seek and] receive praise and honor and glory from one another, and yet do not seek the praise and honor and glory which come from Him**

Who alone is God?" (John 5:44 AMPC). In order to appreciate the faith of the early believers, we must always seek the approval of God and not of men.

4. We cannot throw away the Old Testament scriptures, since it remains the foundation for a maturing faith. Jesus clearly taught that **"until the sky and earth pass away and perish, not one smallest letter nor one little hook [identifying certain Hebrew letters] will pass from the Law until all things [it foreshadows] are accomplished** (Matt 5:18 AMPC).

    For centuries a terrible misunderstanding has pervaded the church. We have preached and taught that God has thrown out the Law and as a result we have seen anarchy, rebellion, and lawlessness in our midst. In some instances new cults have sprung up that parade themselves as "the true followers of Jesus Christ."

5. Lastly, the search for truth may be compared to a man who can only examine the objects of a room from the outside. Through the first glass window he sees the overlay of wicker on the frame of every chair. Through a second he recognizes black mahogany under the overlay of wicker. Through a third the carvings on the back of each chair delight him. Through a fourth he sees that part of each leg is overlaid with enamel. Likewise, scriptures, meditated on for a third or fourth time, may reveal different angles of truth to us. Throughout this study, therefore, repeated scriptures will open up more and more gems of truth that must be held up in the light of God's Word and Spirit so that they may be confirmed as genuine.

    Nor can we forget that the only scriptures the Early Church possessed by which to live were from the Old Testament.

Therefore, Paul, the foremost apostle of the Early church taught, that *"every Scripture is God-breathed (given by God's inspiration) and profitable for instruction, for reproof and conviction of sin, for correction of error and discipline in obedience, [and] for training in righteousness(in holy living, in conformity to God's will in thought, purpose, and action)"* (2 Tim 3:16 AMPC).

Jesus Himself taught, **"If you believed and relied on Moses, you would believe and rely on Me, for he wrote about Me [personally]. But if you do not believe and trust his writings, how then will you believe and trust My teachings? [How shall you cleave to and rely on My words?** (John 5:46.47 AMPC).

In the times of the judges of Israel, men often chose the easy way rather than the perfect will of God (Amos 6:1; Gal 5:16). After the judge was dead, they became more corrupt than their fathers (Judg 2:19 AM PC).

Accepting tradition is certainly easier than searching the scriptures to find the truth which is the only path to freedom.

In His prayer for unity among believers, Jesus declared, **"Your Word is Truth"** (John 17:17). To Jewish believers He declared, **"You will know the Truth, and the Truth will set you free"** (John 8:32).

Jesus once challenged the Pharisees, **"You have a fine way of rejecting [thus thwarting and nullifying and doing away with] the commandment of God in order to keep your tradition (your own human regulations)! Thus you are nullifying and making void and of no effect [the authority of] the Word of God through your tradition, which you [in turn] hand on. And many things of this kind you are doing** (Mark 7:9, 13 AMPC).

May we all be blessed as we search the scriptures diligently!

C. Richard McCaw

FOREWORD

*E*ver since the advent of the Millerite movement of the 1830s to the 1840s, during the period of the Second Great Awakening, leading to the official founding of the Seventh-day Adventist Church in 1863, the Sabbath has become an issue at the center of many ongoing Church-goers debates between "Seventh Day Adventists" and "Sunday Worshippers."

As a pastor and Bible teacher, few experiences are more gratifying than learning that a Christian believer's thesis, note, manual or paper has been accepted for publication. (If the publication is relevant at the local, regional and global levels, so much the better). Few tasks are more satisfying than toiling for months to produce a work whose time has come and, for all the right reasons, is now being published.

While there has been a proliferation of books, manuals, and journals, student notes and comments published, some merely scratched the surface. *The VALUE of Complete REST* is a manual that reflects a unique blend of strong writing skills, comprehensive research, in-depth analysis, and scholarly writing. Known as a trusted Bible teacher, expositor, and dependable theologian, the author offers a thorough yet concise, down-to-earth style, providing "information-at-your fingertips." This is a manual that should prove tremendously helpful and, in many cases, constitute an indispensable tool for studying both Old and New Testament teachings about the Sabbath, helping readers to "identify and connect the dots."

The VALUE of Complete REST includes a carefully structured and open-ended introduction to the fundamentals of both the Biblical and historical perspectives related to the Sabbath as a part of the church's life and lifestyle. The manual weaves together colorful illustrations, Bible-based doctrines and Christ-centered principles to help Bible scholars understand both text and context. They will find the relevance in relating content to intent, and celebrate the application of Scripture to the Sabbath as part of our everyday Christian life.

Bible scholars will be happy to discover the findings that are revealed by the author's process of conceptualizing, researching, organizing, polishing, submitting, and publishing *The VALUE of Complete REST.* They will be blessed as they are edified, empowered, encouraged, and elevated with this gifted teacher and role model's approach to the subject. They will be able also to discover God's purpose, plan, path, and power of the Sabbath in their lives, and the role it plays in fulfilling God's calling, mission, and assignments for their lives.

What I appreciate most about this book is that it guides the reader each step of the way. The author addresses the challenges, and offers comparisons and contrasts that are posed by alternative schools of thought. He also provides various examples of how understanding the Sabbath can benefit the reader who is accurately and adequately informed by the Word, transformed by the Holy Spirit, and is being conformed to the likeness and image of Christ.

I strongly recommend *The VALUE of Complete REST* to Bible students and the Church leaders who mentor them. I can say without reservation that this publication, and, more specifically, the method it espouses should change your life for the better. For more than a dozen years, I have pastored a local church, while simultaneously serving as the Bible Teacher for a number of other churches throughout the New York Tri-State area.

I could stop there, but I would be remiss if, in addressing

the merits of this publication, I failed to mention how much I personally enjoyed reading and reviewing this book.

I am satisfied that readers of this publication will find it a useful tool in:

- Discovering, understanding and evaluating the issues and challenges related to the Sabbath, and how our lifestyles measure up in relation to God's Word and the teachings of the Bible on the subject.

- Enhancing personal spiritual growth, with the ability to identify and evaluate potentially erroneous thinking, and adjust to the correct thinking of God's Word.

- Discovering and understanding how God responds to us, and the dynamics involved in cultivating a quality relationship with Him in relation to the Sabbath.

The VALUE of Complete REST is clear, with easy-to-follow expositions...a treasure trove of vital information...an ideal reference manual for pastors, teachers, students, and personal Bible study... and an absolute "must read" manual.

Rev. Dr. Molendyno G. Moxey
Senior Pastor, New Covenant Community Church-NYC
Queens, New York.
Tel: (646) 379-7290
Email: mgmoxey123@gmail.com

The VALUE of Complete REST - BOOK 1 Finding REST in a Restless Age

Preface

How I came to write this book

*M*any years ago after being ordained as a minister, fellow ministers and I met with a group of Sabbath keepers at a nearby school to debate the Sabbath question. Interested in opposing arguments to enrich my knowledge of the subject, I carefully took notes on every scripture, and later wrote an extensive eighty-five question Bible Study entitled "Another Look at the Sabbath."

As I observed the sense of lawlessness among professing believers, it was obvious that many believed that they were free from the law.

Soon I discovered that many of us were rushing about fulfilling material necessities to the destruction of our spiritual, emotional and physical well-being. Many found themselves floundering in their attachment to the Lord, the major battle being how to find time for being in His presence.

Why I wrote this book

Tremendous prejudice exists today with respect to this subject. We therefore need to search the scriptures more diligently and to interpret them with the correct tools that govern translation and context.

A simple illustration will highlight the problem: a famous quote of Paul, *"Christ is the end of the law,"* in which "end" is wrongly interpreted to mean that Christ "discarded" the law or that the law was "done away" or "ended."

A proper examination of the Greek word "telos" translated "goal" or "purpose" throws a different light upon Paul's words, and helps us to understand that "Christ is the goal of the law" (Rom 10:4).

Therefore, it is my prayer that believers will examine every scripture, lay aside unbiblical, corrosive tradition, and hear what the scriptures really teach and then go out and obey God.

In the following pages will be definite answers to difficult questions that have bothered and confused believers for centuries. Here are some of the questions that must be examined carefully:

How does the scripture define a "day" with respect to the Sabbath question?

Is it true that the Seventh day can only be accepted as the biblical day of rest?

Why did God command the keeping of the Sabbath?

Was the Sabbath given only to the Jews?

Was the Sabbath confined to a specific dispensation?

Did Jesus' coming do away with the Seventh day Sabbath?

Did New Testament believers observe the Sabbath after the resurrection of Jesus Christ?

Did the apostles teach that we should abandon the Ten Commandments, including the Seventh Day Sabbath?

What evidence is there that a man truly loves God?

In this first book, some questions may not be answered but

in the following books. We believe that the inspired Word of God is a lamp for our feet and that light from the Spirit will illuminate our path to find truth that will set us free.

Above all, may we come to know the Lord God intimately.

Sincerely

C. Richard McCaw

SPECIAL NOTE: The names of certain persons have been changed to protect the privacy of individuals in sensitive situations. Dates of events have been examined and are as accurate as possible, despite debates that still exist in the world of archaeology.

DEFINITION OF TERMS:
"Law of God" refers to the Ten Commandments placed INSIDE the Ark of the Covenant (Exod 40:20).

"Law of Moses" refers to the laws, ceremonials and curses for breaking God's commandments, which were placed OUTSIDE IN THE SIDE of the Ark of the Covenant, (Deut 31:26).

"Torah" refers to the first five books of the Bible.

TO THE READER:

If any part of this book appears with typographical or other errors, please contact the author, C. Richard McCaw at richmccaw@netzero.net so that corrections may be made in future editions. Thank you!

Acknowledgements

*T*hanks to the Holy Spirit, Who always inspires me to write. Many have told me how blessed they have been by words He has given me.

A multitude of thanks to My mother, who is now with the Lord, who always encouraged my creative abilities, and constantly read and listened to my poems and stories.

Thanks also to: Fred Morris, former editor of the Caribbean Challenge, who published my testimony, my first short story 'Simon and the Grapes,' and my six-part 'Cary Crusoe teenage serial.'

Caribbean Conference of Churches whose short story contest awarded me a scholarship in 1976 to represent Jamaica at the Caribbean Writers and Artists Conference in Trinidad.

Maxine Pinnock, who published my teenage novel as a monthly serial in her "Impact on Youth" magazine.

Joslyn Smith, Florida International University professor, whose advice greatly helped in the technical aspects of this book. Wilson Wong, who offered excellent suggestions for fascinating changes in text design and other aspects. Homer Slack of "thesharemagazine.com" for the beautiful cover.

Special thanks to Rev. Dr. Molendyno Moxey, who graciously read the manuscript and wrote the Foreword for the series.

C. Richard McCaw

1
Our Desperate Need for Rest

*Y*ears ago, a pastor's wife, exhausted from a long work week and loss of sleep was driving home with her children after a church service. She did not see the truck parked along the road without parking lights on. Suddenly, she slammed head-on and died on the spot.

Our desperate need for rest cannot be simply ignored.

As human beings, we are much like a lamp disconnected from its power source. We have been cut off from the life-giving spiritual source of the Universe. Lost, we wander about searching for a way out of our predicament. Terribly confused and restless, we are not sure what the truth is, so we invent numerous man-made schemes.

This is made more complicated by our modern lifestyle of hurry-sickness. With too many deadlines, and TV continually bombarding us, most of us are stressed out from extreme anxiety. Thoroughly saturated, we switch off the late-night show and stagger into bed.

The importance of proper rest cannot be overestimated. Sleep deprivation can actually take us out of this world and into the next before our time! Adults still need regular bedtime routines. Sleep specialists insist that, as much as possible, we should have a set time to retire each night and begin unwinding an hour or two before.

A single mother may arrive home in the kitchen with bags of groceries that bulge in her arms, and return to her car twice for the remaining bags, then flop down in the kitchen chair completely exhausted.

Caffeine had kept her alert in the morning, in the afternoon and before executive meetings. Depressed about stacks of work still on her desk, she grew more and more anxious about her next projects. As co-workers tried talking to her, she became increasingly irritable. She multitasked from event to event, each more urgent than the last.

On the way home, she raced passed cars, her windows vibrating from their loud stereo systems. At the supermarket in the "ten items only" line she counted people's items, and kept remembering the unreasonable neighbors she would have to face later. She had worked late at night for weeks complaining about things she was never able to do.

When her son shouted from another room in front of the TV, *"Mom, what's for dinner?"* she became aggressive and shouted back in a loud and angry voice, *"Go fix it yourself!"*

Lack of sleep affects children even more than adults, yet many of us allow our children to keep the same late hours as ourselves. When tired or hungry they usually whine and cry.

Imagine a young mother who takes her five-year-old son to a coworker's birthday party at seven-thirty one night and returns home at 10:00 p.m. Next morning, she drags him out of bed at 5:30 a.m. for school. Later that day as she sips coffee with a coworker, she complains, "I don't know why my son keeps whining or throwing tantrums!"

Another six–year-old boy always took his nap at school at 12:00 p.m. But his father took him from school and drove from place to place until almost 4:00 p.m. By then he was so tired, he could not think rationally. When told it was time for a nap, he screamed, *"NO!*

I don't want a nap!" and fought all the way to bed.

Children also need time for a break each day. In summer those too old for naps benefit by 30 minutes each day in their rooms where they can read, color or engage in some quiet activity.

Today's world is filled with much confusion and restlessness. The human heart cries out for a place of real rest and peace that can only come from God.

When I was a child we often visited the Hope Botanical Gardens in Jamaica on Sunday afternoons. Children and even adults would enjoy entering a section called the "Maze."

Calculated to confuse, you could really get lost in the well-designed and cultivated shrub paths that sometimes led to dead ends, and in the burning sun we were hungry, anxious and restless. What a relief when we found ourselves out of the confusion and heat. Some had been going around and around in never-ending circles.

Doctors report that worn out bodies are susceptible to more viruses, and soon become like an old car about to shut down on the road. The world seems like a hazy fog and every task becomes burdensome.

What is all this saying to us? Our bodies were created by a gracious and wise Creator to have consistent and regular routines for activity and rest, without which we become restless and miserable.

Dr. Archibald Hart, in his book "Adrenalin and Stress," pointed out that in spite of a person's theological beliefs about the Sabbath instituted under the Old Covenant, the blessings that come from its strict observance are vast since it protects us from stress, and changes bad stress into good stress. [1]

With so many scheduled activities, many church services are

structured to stimulate and excite rather than to promote prayer and meditation. Adrenalin flows strongly during devotional times and is the same as in the rest of the week. That includes preachers and ministers, who do most of their primary week's work on Sundays!

Our modern world has become increasingly restless and would well heed the words of Jesus Christ: **"Come to Me, all you who labor and are heavy laden, and I will give you rest. Take My yoke upon you and learn from Me, for I am gentle and lowly in heart, and you will find rest for your souls."** [2]

Did God therefore create for us a special, scheduled time as a way of escape from the restlessness of today's world? That is the major question that we will continue to examine in this study before us.

NOTES

[1] Hart, Dr. Archibald. Adrenalin and Stress. Dallas, London, Vancouver, Melbourne: Word Publishing, 1991 p. 34) (paraphrase)

[2] Matt 11:28, 29

2
Rest for the Weary

A large-bodied woman with a great bosom once stood outside a white Toyota Camry, whose back door was open. Her little boy, only 7 years old, stood nearby gazing at a duck that was winging its way over the tops of cars in the supermarket parking lot. She was exhausted after all the shopping, burdened by the thought of the traffic on the way home and that she still had the evening meal to cook.

"Get in the car!" she shouted.

Enthralled by the duck's flight, the little boy did not hear.

"I said get in!" She was in a terrible rage. Shoppers nearby turned their heads.

Finally, with eyes still fixed upon the bird, he slowly crawled into the back seat. Quickly she grabbed the door and slammed it with all the strength her large arms could provide.

Today more than ever you can often observe similar situations very easily, the anxiety addiction that floods people hurrying across the face of the earth.

Many are held in bondage by fear, so that nervous disorders and heart complaints have increased astronomically. Negative news creeps across the TV screen, rattling our nerves and hearts and stimulating depression. To escape the deluge, some of us turn to smoking, alcohol and drugs instead of to God.

The cumulative effect upon today's children and youth cause them to be more negative in their behavior than in previous ages. Restless, they seek more and more material playthings to settle their quest for increasing excitement and emotional satisfaction.

Did our Creator intend that genuine believers should enter into a complete rest away from the emotional, mental and spiritual toil that besets mankind? And on what foundation was such a rest built?

One day the disciples of Jesus asked Him, *"What shall we do, that we may work the works of God?"* [1]

Their question exposes for us the great hindrance to faith. Even some followers of Jesus Christ have this strong sense of WORKING to achieve spiritual results.

However, Jesus brilliantly confronted the problem when He declared, **"This is the work of God, that you *believe* in Him Whom He sent."**

To believe is to abandon all earthly concerns, to cast ourselves completely upon God, and to give ourselves quality time to be with Him. That sense of complete rest is the deepest experience of that special time apart from the world to which He invites everyone who believes in Him.

NOTES

[1] John 6:28-29

3
Our Instinctive need for Love

*V*ery often our restlessness comes from our deep instinctive need to love and be loved.

Here is the testimony of a girl named Tina, who seeking for love, became more and more restless as she desperately sought satisfaction in human relationships.

"Trying to find love occupied most of my time in my later teenage and young adult years. Deeply insecure, I was seeking acceptance and approval and anxiously trying to find my own identity. Very afraid of being alone, I skipped from one relationship to another, slipping further and further away from what I really needed.

Besides my regular job, I ambitiously worked outside on side projects and other interests. However, in every relationship, every important thing in my life fell in the background in order to focus exclusively on the person I was dating. The truth is, I did not respect myself. I felt that finding a lover was the most important thing in my life, in spite of the fact that my passions, purpose, and true self were gradually disappearing from my life.

Infatuation, loneliness, fear of abandonment and the guilt of obligation had been enslaving me in those relationships. I was trapped while seeking love for the wrong reasons, convinced that no one else would ever love me. Although I seemed happy on the outside, my heart was deeply empty."

This young adult was frantically searching for love, believing that another mortal human being could meet her deepest emotional needs.

That mistaken idea has led to some of the saddest stories you

The VALUE of Complete REST - BOOK 1 Finding REST in a Restless Age

may ever hear.

For example, a prominent Newscast broadcasted an account on Jan. 28, 2012 entitled "FORBIDDEN YOUNG LOVE ENDS WITH A MOTHER'S VIOLENT MURDER."

A single mother in EL DORADO HILLS, California, had been having trouble with her fourteen-year-old daughter, who had become romantically involved with a nineteen-year-old college freshman when she was in ninth grade.

"Mom," her daughter may have said, *"He's in desperate need of somewhere to rent."*

The mother probably thought to herself, *"Well, they seem to be just friends."*

Perhaps, her friends asked her, *"Do you know this young man?"*

"No," she must have replied, *"They both told me he's gay! Besides, he can help my daughter with homework and the rent money can help me pay the mortgage."*

"Don't do it!" they warned. But the mother was very strong-willed. In spite of the fact that none of her friends or family wanted him there, she allowed this young man to move in by April. However, by May she had become suspicious.

One day she found them at home in a compromising relationship, her daughter crouched naked inside the closet and covering herself. She then enlisted two of her male co-workers to help throw the young man's things on the sidewalk and warned him, *"If you continue seeing my daughter, I'll call the sheriff!"*

However, despite her threats, he sneaked stealthily into the house twenty times continuing the affair. Enraged, the mother then called in the authorities.

What may have been in the mind of that young man? Perhaps he was thinking, *"I love this girl more than anyone else in the world! Nobody's going to get in my way of having her!"*

What may have been in the mind of that teenager? She may have reasoned, *"He's the only guy that really loves me. I'm not going to let even my mother come between us!"*

From then on the couple plotted to kill anyone who hindered their illicit relationship.

When the parents of that mother heard from her boss that she had not turned up for work one Friday and the following Monday without calling, her parents became alarmed.

Her boss called the sheriff. Then her parents, who were living two miles away, rushed over to her house only to find two sheriff cars and two deputies outside. When the CSI van arrived, about twenty detectives were wandering about the place.

The sad ending to the affair would horrify anyone. That mother had been stabbed twenty times. According to the prosecutor, *"It was a very, very, very gruesome scene. There was a wound that almost decapitated her. Very violent!"*

Bizarre? Yes! That is only one case which demonstrates the lengths to which lost souls will go to satisfy their deep need for love.

These days many more cases turn up of a parent killing a child or a wife a husband in the pursuit of love. However, the root of the problem lies hidden deep in the human heart, where only God should govern its emotions.

In the Dorado Hills incident the actors did not have a godly focus. That mother's focus was the mortgage, and the couple's focus was each other.

When we worship the creature more than the Creator, we have made an idol of the transient and material, and often the damage to our souls is irreparable!

Paul, the apostle, once taught Colossian believers that, *"(Christ) Himself, existed before all things, and in Him all things consist (cohere, are held together). He also is the Head of [His] body, the church; seeing He is the Beginning, the Firstborn from among the dead, so that He alone in everything and in every respect might occupy the chief place [stand first and be preeminent]"* [1]

Since no human being can ever truly satisfy the deepest longings of our souls, we can only turn to the Eternal God of all things and surrender to Him. His love endures forever! That is why the psalmist, David, wrote, *"Oh come, let us worship and bow down; let us kneel before the LORD, our Maker.* [2]

Now all human lovers expect that special time together in order to enrich their relationship. The Eternal God and Eternal Lover of our souls also has selected a special time to meet with us. That special time He has called **"My holy day."** [3]

Did God therefore create a special time once every week to fulfill our deep need of love, through a satisfying relationship with Him? Such an intimate relationship would be just the prescription to fulfill our desperate need to love and be loved.

Embedded deep in the human psyche is the instinct of love which demands love at whatever cost. But we often turn away from the God of the universe, the very source of love, Whom John, the apostle, described in these simple words - God is LOVE.[4]

Therefore, we cannot forget the very first commandment, **"You shall love the Lord your God with all your heart, with all your soul and with all your strength."** [5]

NOTES

[1] Col 1:17, 18 (AMPC)

[2] Psa 85:6

[3] Isa 58:13

[4] 1 John 4:16

[5] Deut 6: 5

4
Our Instinctive Need for Worship

*O*ur restlessness may also come from our deep need for worship.

Created in the image of God, we also have an instinctive need not only for love but also for worship. However, our archenemy is determined to divert the worship of the true God to himself.

Ezekiel, the prophet, has left for us a history of our chief adversary, Lucifer (also called "Satan").

"You were in Eden, the garden of God; every precious stone was your covering; the sardius, topaz, and diamond, beryl, onyx, and jasper, sapphire, turquoise, and emerald with gold. The workmanship of your timbrels and pipes was prepared for you on the day you were created." He could do amazing things! *"You walked back and forth in the midst of fiery stones. You were perfect in your ways from the day you were created, till iniquity was found in you. Your heart was lifted up because of your beauty; you corrupted your wisdom for the sake of your splendor."* [1]

The angel Lucifer wanted to become a god in order to attract the worship of the entire universe to himself. Expelled from heaven, he arrived on earth to tempt everyone to worship him. He knew that every spirit being must worship.

Therefore, when Jesus was fasting in the desert, Satan boasted, *"All this authority I will give You, and their glory; for this has been delivered to me, and I give it to whomever I wish. Therefore, if You will worship before me, all will be Yours."*

But Jesus had come to earth to redeem mankind from bondage to the devil and to restore the worship of His Father. [2]

If an individual does not worship God, the need for worship remains deep and strong. That is why the heathen carve idols, invent and worship myriads of gods. No one can live without worship.

However, the exaltation of anything or anyone apart from God is doomed to destruction from the very start.

Lucifer began to think of himself more highly than he ought, when he began to take over the role of a god.

Ezekiel draws aside the curtain, and we hear God declaring his eternal doom, **"I cast you to the ground. I laid you before kings, that they might gaze at you."**

Think of the great kings of the earth, who saw themselves as all powerful, who pronounced execution at the flick of a finger, who worshipped no one else but themselves.

No longer were these kings arrayed in fine splendor in their palaces, nor waited upon by innumerable servants nor pleasuring in all their fleshly desires. They were in Hell, bereft of fame and future, where torment of mind and soul overwhelmed them. Their evil hearts had not deserted them; forever they would remember with bitterness their judgment and mourn for their past. Suddenly they witnessed the arrival of the one who had deceived them and horror took hold of them.

God had sentenced Lucifer. **"You defiled your sanctuaries by the multitude of your iniquities, by the iniquity of your trading; therefore, I brought fire from your midst; it devoured you, and I turned you to ashes upon the earth in the sight of all who saw you. All who knew you among the peoples are astonished at you; you have become a horror, and shall be no more forever"** [3]

Then Isaiah opens up for us a horrible vista about his fall.

"Hell from beneath is excited about you, to meet you at your coming; it stirs up the dead for you, all the chief ones of the earth; it has raised up from their thrones all the kings of the nations. They all shall speak and say to you: `Have you also become as weak as we? Have you become like us? Your pomp is brought down to Sheol, and the sound of your stringed instruments; the maggot is spread under you, and worms cover you.

"How you are fallen from heaven, O Lucifer, son of the morning! How you are cut down to the ground, you who weakened the nations! For you have said in your heart: 'I will ascend into heaven, I will exalt my throne above the stars of God; I will also sit on the mount of the congregation on the farthest sides of the north; I will ascend above the heights of the clouds, I will be like the Most High.'

Yet, you shall be brought down to Sheol, to the lowest depths of the Pit. Those who see you will gaze at you, and consider you, saying: 'Is this the man who made the earth tremble, who shook kingdoms, who made the world as a wilderness and destroyed its cities, who did not open the house of his prisoners?'"
[4]

God confronted his pride and rebellion, for he should have worshiped the Lord God and served Him alone.

What took place in the spirit of Lucifer can happen to anyone, who refuses to exalt Jesus Christ as King. In our searching for self-esteem we take to ourselves the role of gods.

That is why the Master rebuked the devil by quoting the Torah command: **"It is written, you shall worship the LORD your God, and *Him only* you shall serve."** [5]

That irrevocable law is fixed and unchangeable in the universe, created and governed by the God of Israel. How then can mortal human beings really enter into true worship?

After the Lord manifested Himself to Moses on Mount Sinai, and described in detail the divine attributes of His holiness, Moses immediately bowed his head and worshiped. He had seen and heard the Lord in all His exalted glory proclaiming the divine name and demonstrating true worship.[6]

When the need to worship is not met, often the image of God within us can become so twisted that we begin to exalt ourselves in a desire to be worshiped. This opens doors into the spirit realm for every evil devised by the devil himself, and opposes the fulfillment of God's will in our lives.

God is always seeking true worshippers, and He will not share His glory with any other god. Could it be that He has therefore set apart the Seventh Day of every week, as a special time for us to forget about earthly things and for us to love and to worship Him? That is the question we are seeking to answer.

NOTES

[1] Ezek 28:13-17

[2] Luke 4:6-7

[3] Ezek 28:18

[4] Isa 14:9-17

[5] Luke 4:8

[6] Exod 34:1-8

Sheol refers to the invisible world of departed spirits (Hebrew: "the all-demanding world" = Greek: Hades, "the unknown region"). In the Hebrew Scriptures this meant the place of darkness, the abode of the dead, both of the righteous and the wicked – (sometimes translated "Hell").

5
The Danger of Ignorance

*W*hether in science or principles of behavior, ignorance cannot be allowed to prevail. No relationship can survive, whether human or divine, where a lack of knowledge is allowed to have full sway. This is especially dangerous if a believer hopes to have a deep and loving relationship with God.

In the 18th century, the danger of ignorance was clearly demonstrated in the medical profession in the following incidents.

In 1675 Anton van Leeuwenhoek with the invention of the microscope was the first to discover microorganisms, or life forms invisible to the naked eye. However, ignorance still prevailed in the scientific community for nearly 200 years as scientists saw no connection between microbes and disease.[1]

In 1747 James Lind, a young Scottish naval surgeon may have been unable to sleep one night and risen from bed, as the ship on which he was traveling charted its way through the high seas. Deeply troubled by the fact that many sailors on board had already succumbed to scurvy, perhaps he thumbed through medical journals in an effort to find some solution. [2]

He must have thought to himself. *"There must be a cure for this dreadful disease."*

For four centuries medical ignorance of scurvy, caused by a severe lack of vitamin C had been the cause of the medical distress. About two hundred and seventy years ago, James Lind did something truly revolutionary.

On May 20, 1747, he took twelve sailors under his care for scurvy and divided them into six groups. He gave the first group a quart of cider a day; the second a dose of a royal navy patent medicine; the third he treated with vinegar; the fourth with nutmeg, and the fifth with ordinary saltwater - accepted treatments for scurvy at the time. For the sixth group he prescribed two oranges and a lemon each day, another suggested cure.

At sea, he had invented the clinical trial, and the results were spectacular. After six days the last group returned fit for duty and service, while the others showed no marked improvement. However, in 1747 when James Lind discovered that scurvy was caused by a severe deficiency of vitamin C, the scientific community, because of ignorance, made no changes in their treatment of the disease.

From the time of Hippocrates to that of Louis Pasteur, the medical profession persisted in a plausible yet mistaken view that disease was spontaneously generated instead of being created by microorganisms that grow by reproduction.

During that period if you had been seriously ill, a doctor would have made an incision with a knife on your arm, and even if you had grimaced, you would have been bled (a system of drawing blood to get rid of the bad blood believed to have been the root of the problem). Or he may have used other remedies accepted at that time. It was also common practice for doctors to wear a filthy butcher's apron, unwittingly spreading your infection to the next patient.

In 1847 Ignaz Semmelweis, a Hungarian obstetrician, was working at Vienna's Allgemeines Krankenhaus. Soon he observed many deaths from puerperal fever as doctors and medical students helped women in the hospital delivery room. However, he noticed that births attended by the midwives were relatively safe.[3]

On further investigation Semmelweis realized that physicians usually arrived directly from autopsies, and concluded that germs from the autopsies were the real problem. Semmelweis then insisted that doctors wash their hands with chlorinated lime water before examining pregnant women.

Noticeably the childbirth deaths dramatically fell from 18% to 2.2% at his hospital. However, when he made those astounding discoveries, most of the Viennese medical establishment, because of the prevailing ignorance, viciously attacked him and his theories.

During the 1854 cholera outbreak in Soho, London, John Snow's statistical analysis of affected cases identified that the disease had been transmitted by drinking water from the Broad Street pump, and that the outbreak was not consistent with the current scientific miasma theory. Once again, ignorance had governed the scientific community.[4]

Louis Pasteur, a Frenchman (1822-1895), then Dean of the Faculty of Science at the University of Lille, explored the mysterious world of germs.[5]

One day a man, who worked at a factory that produced beer from sugar beets, approached him lamenting that vats of the fermented beer were turning sour. He then asked Pasteur, *"Sir, can you find out the cause of this problem?"*

Using a microscope to analyze beer samples, Pasteur found thousands of microorganisms. His theory was that "microbes" or "germs" were not the result of the beer going sour, rather they were the cause. Pasteur went on to study other liquids such as vinegar and milk.

From further experiments Pasteur discovered and accurately declared that the air contained tiny living organisms unseen by the naked eye that caused putrefaction of liquids, which could be prevented by killing them with heat.

However, in 1872 when he made that discovery, Pierre Pachet, Professor of Physiology at Toulouse, made the scathing remark, *"Louis Pasteur's theory of germs is ridiculous fiction."*

Between 1879 and 1900 doctors discovered that infectious diseases were caused by microscopic organisms called germs. That discovery led to safe surgery, large–scale vaccination programs, great improvements in hygiene and sanitation, and the pasteurization of dairy products, but above all, the emergence of antibiotic medicine.

In 1982 Stanley Prusiner (born 1942) discovered that disease could be caused by a class of infectious proteins (not containing a nucleus) which he termed "prions." [6]

Prusiner, at first, received much skepticism from the scientific community. However, in 1997 he was awarded the Nobel Prize for his work. The proteins cause scrapie in sheep, mad cow disease, and spongiform diseases such as Creutzfeldt-Jakob disease in humans. Currently there is no cure for this disease.

From Galileo's discovery that the earth revolves around the sun, to the Soviet suppression of the study of genetics under Stalin, to the claims that tobacco companies made for years that cigarette smoking and cancer could not be linked, human beings have often failed to investigate the truth and have rejected knowledge that might have saved countless lives.

NOTES

[1] https://en.wikipedia.org/wiki/Anton_Leeuwenhoek 19 Jan 2016

[2] https://en.wikipedia.org/wiki/James_Lind 11 Jan. 2016

[3] https://en.wikipedia.org/wiki/Ignaz_Semmelweis 27 Jan. 2016

[4] https://en.wikipedia.org/wiki/John_Snow_(physican) 13 Jan. 2016

[5] https://en.wikipedia.org/wiki/Louis_Pasteur 13 Jan.2016

[6] www. Britannica.com/biography/Stanley-B-Pruisiner 15 Jan 2016

6
The Consequences of Ignorance

*W*hen ignorance prevailed over the medical profession, and scurvy ravaged distraught sailors what horror must have faced many a doctor and many a suffering sailor at sea! A doctor may have stood close by as the disease ravaged his distressed patient.

A short, small-bodied nurse may have heard of James Lind's experiment and remarked, *"Doctor, haven't you read what James Lind did to the sailors under his care? Why don't you try it? It may be just the thing to save this poor man's life!"*

However, although the doctor knew of Lind's successful experiment, and the medical profession's sharp criticisms, he would have been embarrassed and confused. Removing his pince-nez, he may have wiped his perspiring forehead and answered, *"If I try the same thing and it doesn't work, they'll all think me a quack!"*

The nurse may have sent up a prayer to the Lord or the Virgin Mary, *"Have mercy, Lord*!" or "*Mother of God, pray for us*!" In spite of her prayer, the poor sailor would have begun to breathe his last. Not too long afterwards, he was gone!

The doctor was in bondage to ignorance, fear and self-interest, while death reigned right before him.

When James Lind in 1747 discovered that a severe deficiency of vitamin C caused scurvy, his treatment was not put into practice in the royal navy until 1795, more than four decades after the publication of his treatise, and a year after his death. Between those crucial years countless sailors continued to die every year.

During the period when the medical profession believed in bleeding patients, had the doctor bled one patient and then seen you afterwards, he may have brought some disease and you would have died.

If you were a woman delivering a baby in 1847, when Ignaz Semmelweis was investigating why so many mothers and their babies were dying, if a midwife had attended to you, you and your newborn may have escaped with your life. But if a doctor had come from an autopsy, germs from a corpse would have disposed of you for your relatives to weep over and to bury you.

Now observe carefully how a lack of knowledge can destroy the wellbeing of many people and note this unbelievably ever recurring theme: humans are not always as smart as they would like to believe.

Although some believe that "ignorance is bliss," numerous incidents have proven the saying to be far from true! Many a man during his formative years idled his hours away, refusing to apply himself diligently to acquire knowledge, and today he stands by the roadside with a placard that reads: WILL WORK FOR FOOD.

The message remains consistent throughout the scriptures. Ignorance cannot be allowed to have sway over our minds. Many of us have been trapped by unbiblical traditions for a long time, because we have been ignorant of the Word of God. That is why God wants time with us, so that we might not remain ignorant of His laws and ways and suffer the consequences of moral and spiritual destruction.

Perhaps God did establish from the foundation of the world a definite schedule, a weekly routine to ensure time with us. He knew the danger and consequences of ignorance and that knowing His laws and ways was paramount in His relationship with us. He also knew that relationships only developed through time, and not just scattered time, but concentrated, protracted and meditative time in the presence of one dearly beloved.

Time with God will cause us to mature spiritually as we come to know Him intimately as the God who separates us from sin.

Nevertheless, no one can attain that deeper relationship with Him without a knowledge of His laws. No one can grow to know Him without adequate time spent in His presence until His thoughts become our thoughts and His ways become our ways.

As the Great Lawgiver of the universe, perhaps God did create that special, separated day, so that we would not need to create our own laws and traditions. At this point, it is reasonable to conclude that He did want us to experience true freedom and joy, as we establish an intimate relationship with Him.

As we continue our research how can we allow ignorance to prevail over us? Have we not seen how those who remain ignorant of God's laws set the stage for their own moral and spiritual destruction? If we love the Lord, let us seek to obey His commandments and thus be blessed.

7
The Danger of Unbiblical Traditions

*S*ometimes our inner restlessness comes from unquestioned rituals and traditions handed down from generation to generation. Somehow, although we cannot explain it, we sense some imbalance or injustice in the practice of such procedures.

Phileas Fogg, the chief protagonist in Jules Verne's novel, "Around the world in 80 Days," confronted such a dreadful tradition.

He may have been lounging at ease in his British club reading the local newspapers, when he overheard a discussion and made a bet of 20,000 pounds that he could travel around the world in 80 days. The men standing around accepted the challenge, and soon Fogg was off on his world tour along with his faithful French servant, Passepartout.

Sometime afterwards, the sound of large elephant's feet could be heard thumping through the Indian forest. As a native guide led them at a rapid pace from the hamlet of Kolby in India, a Brahmin procession began to approach and the guide warned them to hide in a thicket. Quietly they watched as the religious procession with an image of Kali, the goddess of love and death, drew even nearer.

"It's a suttee," said the guide, "a human sacrifice, and is usually voluntary. The woman will be burned alive tomorrow at dawn with her husband, the prince's corpse." After the procession had passed, the guide continued, "This one is not voluntary. The woman did not resist, because they had intoxicated her with fumes of hemp and opium."

Aristobolus of Cassandreia, a Greek historian, who traveled with the expedition of Alexander the Great, recorded the tradition of suttee at the city of Taxila in India. In 316 BC, after an Indian soldier's death in the army of Eumenes of Cardia, voluntary co-cremation appeared later when two wives vied to die on his funeral pyre.[1]

Suttee is an Indian tradition that is often described as voluntary, although in some cases it may have been forced. In one account, the widow seems to have been drugged with bhang opium, and was then tied to the pyre to keep her from fleeing after the fire was lit. In the history of Rajasthan royal funerals have sometimes included the deaths of many wives and concubines.

Today unbiblical tradition is often a great obstacle even in the lives of professing believers. Someone may argue, *"How can I lay aside the traditions of my parents and ancestors, or those of my religion which I have practiced for so long?"*

In certain cults and heathen religions, to abandon the traditions of your forefathers can alienate your entire family. In others it can mean execution.

Since Feb 23, 2012 there has been media reports that Youcef Nadarkhani, 34, was arrested on charges of apostasy more than two years before. At one time an Iranian court sentenced him to death by hanging because he had defied a request by the Gilan provincial court in Rasht, Iran, to repent. The married father-of-two was detained in his home city of Rasht in October 2009, while attempting to register his church. Since those reports, other news have been circulating that he has been released.[2]

Breaking away from religious traditions can certainly stir the anger of cold, unloving hearts.

During the ministry of Christ a woman, afflicted for eighteen years with a spirit of infirmity, whose back was bent and who could not lift up herself, came one day into the synagogue. [3]

The moment Jesus saw her, He called her to him and declared, **"Woman you are loosed from your infirmity!"**

When He laid His hands upon her, immediately her back was made straight and she began to praise the Lord.

However, the leader of the synagogue became indignant because Jesus had healed on the Sabbath, and said to the crowd, *"There are six days on which work ought to be done; so come on those days and be cured, and not on the Sabbath day!"*

Jesus then turned to him and rebuked him, **"You hypocrite!"**

His tradition had prevented him from loving his neighbor as he loved himself. If his ox or donkey had been thirsty, he would have led it from the stall to be watered. Obviously, he had more compassion for an animal than for a fellow human being. Tradition had blinded his eyes from seeing the truth of God's Word.

Today God is calling us to lay aside every unbiblical tradition and to obey Him with all our hearts.

NOTES

[1] wikipedia.org/wiki/Sutee 20 Jan 2016

[2] https://en.wikipedia.org/wiki/Youcef_Nadarkhani 20 Nov 2015

[3] Luke 13:14

8
Spiritual Death-Traps

*P*hileas Fogg gazed upon the death-trap of a suttee, on which men were preparing the fire at the base of a funeral pyre. The horror of the victim's fate weighed heavily upon him. Since they were twelve hours ahead of schedule. he decided that he would attempt to rescue the unfortunate wife that was to be burnt alive with her dead husband.

Fogg heard that the woman was the daughter of a rich Bombay merchant, forced to marry against her will to an old raja. When he died, she escaped, but was captured and condemned by the raja's relatives to suttee. Eventually, she was placed upon the funeral pyre, and completely surrounded by guards. Immediately as it was torched, the oil-soaked wood burst into flames.

Suddenly, in the dark of the night Passepartout could watch no longer, and taking a desperate risk, leapt upon the pyre. Quickly he picked up the woman and brought her down as terrified soldiers and priests closed their eyes, believing that the raja had come to life and delivered his wife. Finally, on the large elephant they raced under a hail of bullets and arrows until they reached Allahabad several hours later and caught a train to Calcutta.

Imagine that you had visited the home of one of the guards and asked, *"Don't you see how cruel such a religious tradition is?"*

He would have replied, *"Yes, but we have been practicing that ritual for centuries! The raja needs his wife in the next life. How would he manage without her?"*

Years of religious tradition would have blinded his spiritual eyes.

"Tradition" is usually taken to be an obstacle to reform.

Traditional societies are assumed to be reluctant to change, or worse, harbor nostalgic notions of returning to some mythical golden age.

Now listen to this. One day a pastor was preparing more than 20 people for baptism by the seaside in the warm Jamaican climate. A cool and gentle breeze blowing in under tall palm trees from across the sea may have caressed them. A young man stood in the crowd watching as candidates were placed under the water and came up lifting their hands and praising God.

Since he had indicated his desire to be baptized, the pastor looked at him several times and asked, *"Are you ready now?"* But each time he replied, *"Not yet, Pastor!"*

Some years later, they met one night at the home of one of the pastor's relatives. After sharing the scriptures, the pastor asked, *"Do you believe the Word of God?"*

"I do, I do!" the young man confidently replied.

Then the pastor reminded him, *"Years ago you wanted to be baptized. Have you since obeyed the Lord in the waters of baptism?"*

"Pastor, I'd prefer not to talk about it!" he replied, *"The priest told me that I was baptized as a baby!"*

Bound by fear of a religion and its leaders, he preferred to disobey God's Word, keep his tradition and to please men.

One day the Pharisees saw that Jesus' disciples had not ritually washed their hands before eating, so they asked the Lord, *"Why do Your disciples not order their way of living according to the tradition handed down by the forefathers [to be observed], but eat with hands unwashed and ceremonially not purified?"*

Jesus rebuked them with these very perceptive words, **"You have a fine way of rejecting [thus thwarting and nullifying and doing away with] the commandment of God in order to keep your tradition (your own human regulations)!"** [1]

Following Jesus is not like joining a fan club, nor is it like becoming one of His admirers. No! Jesus challenges us, **"Whoever of you does not forsake all that he has, cannot be My disciple"** [2]

We face a definite choice: *Will we follow our own way, perhaps the traditions of many years, or will we follow the King of the universe?*

We must diligently seek the truth, and not comfortably follow others who accept teachings not rooted in the scriptures. Nor should we cling to denominational traditions with an attitude that screams, *"My church teaches this, and that's what I believe!"*

If we are to live in the presence of the Most High God, we cannot remain ignorant of His will. Otherwise, we will be swept away with the ungodly and become lost in the crowds. At a preacher's invitation, we may have stepped forward and prayed, and therefore believe that such a response was sufficient to live for God while we stubbornly pursue our own goals.

Serving Jesus Christ involves the taking up of a cross, the denial of the love of material things and the enshrining of Jesus Christ as Supreme Conqueror of our desires. We cannot make Him our servant to provide material things for us. Such an attitude reveals that selfish interests are still on the throne of our lives and manifests as "My will be done on earth!"

Jesus once predicted, **"Many will say to Me in that day, Lord, Lord, have we not prophesied in Your name, cast out demons in Your name, and done many wonders in Your name? And then I will declare to them, 'I never knew you; depart from me, you who practice lawlessness."** [3]

Many of us have been brain-washed by religious dogma and unbiblical traditions that prevent us from enjoying the blessings that God has lovingly promised.

The vision of souls facing eternity without God should stir every believer's heart to reach out beyond the walls of tradition to save all who would willingly surrender to the Lordship of Christ.

Without God at the helm of our lives, unbiblical traditions instilled from our youth can easily destroy us! Let us find for ourselves those traditions and laws that God has instituted through Christ. One clearly defined biblical tradition was that **"The seventh day is the Sabbath belonging to the Lord your God."** [4]

"Did God create a cyclic seventh day rest so that not only the Israelites, but all mankind would be delivered from the bondage of their own unbiblical laws and traditions? Could Jesus' declaration that **"The Sabbath was made for man,"** provide us with a clue to the answer to that question.

NOTES

[1] Mark 7:7 (AMPC)

[2] Luke 14:33

[3] Matt 7:22-23

[4] Exod 20:10

[5] Mark 2:28

9
Our Instinctive Need for Law

*C*ould our restlessness also spring out of a deep inner need for some governing law to keep us on the right path?

News headlines below some time ago provide examples and evidence that each of us has an instinctive need for law in our lives.

"Mom decapitates two-year-old child, then kills herself; nine-year-old boy kidnapped and shot as sister watches; twin sisters brutally murder Mom; eighteen-year-old father rapes and beats his eight-day-old baby, cracking its skull; ten-year-old boy imprisoned for throwing rocks and a brick at a homeless man which severely injured him and left him blind in one eye."

Today modern society is repeating the same sins that destroyed nations in ancient days. When the human heart rejects God's laws, terrible things happen. According to the Index of Leading Cultural Indicators, since 1960 violent crime has increased more than 500 percent and the U.S. has outstripped all industrialized countries in the world.

The effect of lawlessness on young people today is not surprising, since we have removed prayer and the Bible from the classroom and the Ten Commandments from our court rooms. In America we have reached the place where many believe that we can achieve supreme happiness without God, Bible, church or absolute moral standards.

Lawlessness has become acceptable to many people. Children despise the authority of their parents, wives, that of their husbands, employees, that of their employers, and citizens, that of their rulers. Not only do they disobey their superiors, but they will not recognize anyone to whom honor and obedience are due!

Lawlessness like a nasty fog covers the world, so that many cannot distinguish right from wrong. ***"Whoever sins is guilty of breaking God's law, because sin is a breaking of the law*** (GNT).[1]

Herein, therefore is one of our most serious problems: the failure to recognize the deep need of the human heart to submit to law and order, firstly to God's law, then to righteous and just laws established by those whom He has delegated to rule over us.

In addition, one of the saddest observations of today's modern world is that the people who should be upholding the law are often the very ones not only breaking the law but collaborating with others to break the law.

NOTES

[1]   John 3:4 (KJV)

10
The Fruit of Lawlessness

*I*n our own time the moral fabric of society has seriously disintegrated, so that even the young have little or no shame when breaking God's law.

On November 3, 1981, after a sixteen-year-old boy had raped and strangled to death a fourteen-year-old school girl in Milpitas, California, he then drove his pickup truck to nearby hills and dumped her body in a ravine. Later, it was reported that he boasted about her death at school and showed at least ten people the body.[1]

Throughout the world, urban violence is also exploding in the rapidly growing cities of Latin America, Asia, and in the European capitals where communist rule has been overthrown.

Political upheavals in Africa and the Middle East have terrified and angered millions at the apparently endless bloodshed. Criminals are utilizing sophisticated weapons everywhere more and more, and people feel helpless as they sense that political leaders are unable to stem the tide of killing.[2]

Since the end of apartheid in South Africa, public disorder and crime has shown its ugly head everywhere. In Cape Town it is reported that a serious crime takes place every seventeen seconds. If you own a fine car in South Africa, that is risky business. Unemployed thugs often surround such cars at intersections. Then they drag out the occupants, beat them mercilessly and leave them groaning on the roadside with swollen eyes and other bruises. As the car speeds away, its tires screech around the next corner on their way to a "joy ride." Found later, it would have been vandalized or wrecked.[3]

The institution of marriage has also been overturned.

Fornication has now become acceptable behavior. Parents and schools now distribute contraceptives to students. Putting away one's spouse, and taking another's mate is now so prevalent that it is taken for granted. Lust is taught in the media and advertisement world as a means of attracting customers to various products.

One outstanding evidence why so many are finding their love for God being blown out by the winds of iniquity is the growing desecration of what some call the Lord's day just as the ungodly world: to pursue pleasure, sports, shopping and sightseeing, and many work in direct violation of the fourth commandment. Attendance at worship services becomes infrequent; and many never make the second service on Sunday. Many watch sports for several hours on their televisions and shorter services indicate that we have become lovers of pleasure more than lovers of God.

No wonder our young people are confused in the maze of conflicting religious dogma and in the moral decline of a nation that once founded its moral standards upon the Judeo-Christian ethics of the Holy Scriptures. Those standards were built upon the laws God gave to His people and which became the spiritual traditions that have preserved human society for many generations. They were founded on scheduled time spent with God. Through ignorance and rebellion the Lord's Day has been laid aside, and restlessness, confusion and violence have taken its place.

NOTES

[1-3] www.jeremiahproject.com/prophecy/lawlessness.html

11
Divine Orders

*W*e may argue at this time that the cycle of the seventh day set apart for rest was only a law for a particular time and a particular nation.

Is there any further evidence of definite cycles that God has established anywhere else?

Probably one day King Solomon said to his wife, *"Honey, I've just discovered something else!"*

She put down the shadow brush she was using to paint under her eyes. *"Schlomo, what's it this time?"*

"I discovered a cycle in the relation of the earth to the sun!" he may have replied. *"I also found that the wind operates in cycles! And there's more!"*

"Tell me!"

"The rivers have a circuit too!" he added excitedly and observed, ***"The wind goes to the south and circles about to the north; it circles and circles about continually, and on its circuit the wind returns again, and all the rivers run into the sea, yet the sea is not full. To the place from which the rivers come, to there and from there they return again."*** [1]

Imagine what would happen if all the rivers did not run into the sea, but leaked off somewhere else into the atmosphere of the universe. Then there would be drought everywhere on earth.

You may have been busy attending to business, your family or investing in the stock market with the hope of one day making it rich.

Perhaps you never noticed the lack of rain, and the creeping heat overtaking the earth.

Imagine one morning a man awakes to discover that his entire garden has withered away. His mouth drops open as he rushes inside to ask his wife if the handyman had not come last week.

She replies, *"Honey, I was so busy that I never saw him."*

Later, while looking over her favorite flower garden outside she noticed that all the lilies had wilted, and her mouth also drops open. Yes, there was drought everywhere. The rivers had not run into the sea and cycled round its circuit to form rain to water the earth.

Solomon once wrote, ***"To everything there is a season and a time to every purpose under the heaven."*** [2]

Imagine one of our early ancestors, a strong elderly man, his jaws sunk in, a bitter look on the corners of his mouth, as he is about to leave the cave (according to the evolutionist) to go hunting one morning.

"Oh, my!" he exclaims. *"It's really cold outside!"* He shivers and hobbles back inside to his wife, and says, *"Gimme that!"* and grabs the bear fur she has wrapped around her. *"You don't need that in here! I've got to hunt food! There's white flakes falling all around outside!"*

She ignores the arthritis in her knees and while wrapping her arms around herself she hurries as fast as she can and sees light snowfall outside. *"Oh, dear! Hurry back! I'll die if you don't come back quickly with another bear fur!"*

They had already seen spring, the hot summer, and autumn with leaves turning brown and falling off the trees. Now they were again seeing the first signs of winter.

As far back in time as scientists have investigated, the cycles of the seasons have always existed. God has established everything in order with consistent regularity. Even the most diehard atheistic scientist will admit, *"Night and day, spring summer, autumn and winter have always existed and still exist!"*

An examination of scripture reveals that a Supermind must have constructed definite cycles in nature and in human emotions and activity.

Now if you go back to listening more closely to the conversation playing out between Solomon and his wife, you would hear her say, *"Schlomo, you told me what you wrote about human emotions, how we all have a time to weep and a time to laugh, a time to mourn and a time to dance, a time to embrace and a time to refrain from embracing, a time to love and a time to hate, a time for war and a time for peace. It's fascinating!"* [3]

"Hey, honey," he would laugh, *"I know it's exciting, but slow down...Isn't it amazing? God has placed cycles in our bodies too!"*

Researchers inform us that we become hungry according to regular ninety minute cycles. Women experience regular menstrual cycles, besides monthly mood swings associated with such cycles. Generally, menstruating women feel best during the first half of their cycle and worse during the second half, just prior to menstruation. Their bodies demand rest and must be replenished.

Men also undergo a weight change of about one or two

pounds, and a regular rhythmic change in the growth of their beards each month. Evidence also points to monthly emotional cycles in men.

Hormones in men also rise and fall in roughly a thirty-day rhythm.[4]

Obviously, God has deposited natural mechanisms within the entire creation that demand definite cycles of rest. Therefore, breaking that divine order cannot be side-stepped for any reason without serious consequences. Sometimes lack of regular rest may not take our own lives, but the lives of innocent people around us, as in the following incident.

In October 2012 in Louisiana State, two elderly people from New Orleans were killed. The male victim had pulled over and was attempting to help the occupants of a Nissan Altima on the side of the highway because of mechanical problems. The female victim was in the back seat of the Altima. A vehicle traveling south struck the Altima from behind, pushing it off the highway. Five others suffered injuries in the two-vehicle accident.[5]

The cause of that terrible accident: Fatigue! Lack of sufficient sleep caused the driver to veer onto the shoulder of Interstate 310, killing two innocent people and bringing distress to several families.

"God is not a God of confusion and disorder, but of peace and order." [6]

In God's system, laws govern everything, and everything goes around and around in consistent cycles: birth, growth, death; seasons every year: spring, summer, autumn and winter.

Is there is a time every week that our Creator has set aside for us to forget all created things and to meet with Him? And did He really designate that time **"My holy Day?"** [7]

Let us go on to discover the truth for ourselves.

NOTES

[1] Eccl 1:5 -7

[2] Eccl 3:1

[3] Eccl 3:4, 8

[4] Perry. Susan & Dawson, Jim. Secrets our Body Clock Reveals. New York: Rawson Book club edition, 1988. p 22, 85, 118 and p 121

[5] http://www.fox8live.com/story/19755316/early-morning-crash-on-i-310-leaves-two-dead-and-multiple-injured

[6] 1 Cor 14:33

[7] Isa 58:13

12
Cycles of Rest

*T*he speaker began at exactly 7:30 p.m. on a rainy Wednesday night. In the packed auditorium chairs filled some of the aisles and people were standing against the back wall.

Although Tom was a strong young adult of about twenty-eight, he was exhausted after a hard day delivering fire equipment all around South Miami. He was still cheery-faced when his large arms hugged his intellectually-inclined wife. She was a beautiful young woman, three years his junior, who wore her attractive dark brown hair on either side of her rouged cheeks with a fashionable hat on her head.

She had persuaded him to drive from the Miami University where she lectured in Science, straight to Orlando to hear an acclaimed scientist lecture on the subject of "Evolution." The moderator had promised the audience that by 9:30 p.m. the closing comments would have been complete.

At 9:00 p.m., Tom leaned back and yawned. The speaker rambled on. He reminded him of a photo of Friedrich Nietzche he had seen on the internet with his large moustache and a good crop of hair on the top of his head. His booming sing-song voice and staccato sentences added to his monotonous tone.

By 9:30 p.m, Tom's eyes began to flicker. People began looking at each other. At 9:45 Tom began to nod and jerked his head left and right to keep from nodding off, since he knew that his wife beside him would be dreadfully embarrassed if he began snoring among those illustrious intellectuals.

But the speaker became carried away with his own eloquence

and kept droning on and on about the same things. Tom tried staring at the wall photos behind the speaker in order to keep his mind alert

He even tried to widen his eyes. At 10:00 o'clock the speaker grew more verbose, throwing out long scientific terms that were lost to Tom. Tom struggled to concentrate. His wife nudged him. He made one final effort to keep sleep from overtaking him completely.

By 10:15 he was gone, and the dreadful had happened. Great sawing sounds of snoring overtook the audience. His wife hid her face in her hands. A few people began rising to leave. The moderator crept up behind the scientist and whispered in his ear. The conclave broke up. Tom's wife poked him in the side and pulled at his sleeve. She almost literally dragged him out of the hall.

Suddenly, for a moment Tom realized that he was sitting beside his wife. As she spun the car around, the tires screeched, and they raced home with a sound like the sawing of wood. His wife burst out laughing.

That meeting had continued way beyond the time allotted and the cycles of nature began to take over. You could almost hear the body and soul of that husband shouting out to him each time he shook his head trying to remain awake, *"We **demand** to rest! We **demand** to rest **RIGHT NOW!** Right Now!"* Nature began screaming, *"We're going on strike **RIGHT NOW!"*** Then it was too much for him. He had entered the sweet world of sleep!

Researchers have determined that our minds operate in ninety minute concentration cycles.[1]

Without a doubt our mortal frames do function in definite ordered cycles! King David once declared, *"He knows our frame; He remembers that we are dust."* [2]

God has constructed us to concentrate for a certain length of time. Have you ever noticed that when listening to a speaker your brain needs to rest after so much knowledge has been imparted to you? We are not created to keep going all the time.

Visit any preschool and observe children outside during the mid-morning break. Hear the screams of delight as they climb up and down the slide, and chase each other around the playground. Watch as they return to the classroom with their bodies invigorated, their brains stimulated by the rest from concentrated listening and study.

School teachers know that students need regular times of refreshing within each day's schedule. The body needs food to eat. The mind needs time to rest. If not, concentration will be lost and distractions become the attraction as their thoughts wander away.

Biologists also confirm the existence of inner body rhythms of temperature and blood pressure. The temperature of our bodies does not remain constant all the time. In fact, regular adjustments of cold and heat appear in cycles as well. Every day the temperature of the human body rises and then falls a degree or two with accurate precision. If we remain in bed all day, our temperature will follow its regular daily cycle.

Under normal circumstances blood pressure also functions in regular cycles having a regular up-and-down rhythm that can vary throughout the day by as much as 20 percent.[3]

In the 1950s sleep researchers first discovered that every ninety minutes adults shift back and forth between deep sleep and dream sleep. Other shorter cycles within each day called ultradian cycles, specifically, the mysterious ninety-minute rhythms, also affect our alertness and habits.

Since the human mind is more alert during dream sleep,

researchers have ascertained that the sleep cycle was only part of a continuous daily alertness and sleepiness rhythm. Every ninety minutes, whether awake or asleep, our alertness rises and falls, and our bodies undergo subtle changes in brain wave patterns, eye movement and muscle tone, that cause us to daydream. These cycles also affect sleepiness, going to the restroom and the urge to eat.

In the creation account, we see that each day accomplished distinct purposes until the work was complete. God was satisfied that man was created and well provided for by having food to eat, night to sleep and a garden in which to labor during the day.

Whenever men rebel against God's laws, whether spiritual, emotional, psychological or physical, they reap the dreadful consequences.

When King Saul decided to go his own way and not obey the instructions that God had given him through Samuel, the prophet, all his prayers and sacrifices to God were a waste of time. He could no longer hear from God. Then he turned to demonic forces by visiting a witch, a thing God had specifically forbidden. By the next day, Saul was a dead man and so were his three sons. [4]

Science and psychology attest to the value of each amenity that God has given man. Without work man's emotional sense of balance becomes warped. Without food his body lacks vitality and becomes sick. Without sleep he becomes not only weary, but nervous and irritable.

Therefore, we observe that God has planned the cycle of night and day to provide a balance of work and rest. Did He not also institute Sabbath rest at the end of every six days, when He set that day apart and called it "**My holy day**"? [5]

We can now conclude that He was indeed wise and gracious

to separate every **Seventh Day** and thus provide all that we need for life and godliness!

NOTES

[1] Perry. Susan & Dawson, Jim. Secrets our Body Clock Reveals. New York: Rawson Book club edition, 1988. p. 22

[2] Psa 103:14

[3] Perry Susan & Dawson,...Ibid. p 6

4 1 Samuel 28 and 31:1-6

[5] Isa 58:13

13
Defining the Lord's Day

*L*ightning. thunder and the sounds of flames of fire burst forth on Mount Sinai. Israelites stood terrified some distance from the mountain, because barriers had been set up to prevent anyone from climbing up to see the inexplicable glory of the God of Israel.

After declaring the first three commandments, the same awesome voice sounded forth, which was very specific.

"The SEVENTH DAY is the Sabbath of the Lord your God."

There was no cloudiness about which day God had selected from the seven days of the week to be His holy day. From the creation of the world the SEVENTH DAY was the only day designated by God in which man should rest which He called the Sabbath.[1]

When the Lord God created the heavens and the earth, the earth was without form and an empty waste, and darkness was upon the face of the very great deep. At that time the Spirit of God hovered over the surface of the waters, and God began to bring order and form into the universe by the word of His power.

"Let there be light!" He said, and light shone forth. God saw that the light was excellent, and then He separated the light from the darkness.[2]

God in His infinite knowledge, wisdom and understanding of the passage of time, was aware of sin's devastating effects on the human personality and ordered the corrective measure. Although the Lord gave the Sabbath command later in written form on tablets of stone to Moses, we cannot forget that the Seventh Day Sabbath was blessed and set apart from the other days of the week long before the Sinai event and directly after God had finished the creation of the heavens and the earth.[3]

Now, we may have some quarrel or complaint with the Creator of the universe, who instituted that definition. We may be like the modern independent intellectual who loves to argue. We may even have been brought up to believe that each individual should determine their own theological doctrine and that none of us ought to impose our personal views on anyone else.

Consider carefully then the dangerous position into which we are placing ourselves. Let us ask ourselves what authority we have to be engaging in such a challenge with the Omnipotent Creator of the universe.

God set the example, and like our Master, Jesus Christ, we should follow His example.[4]

The psalmist David beautifully described God's loving care in his most beloved psalm, *"The LORD is my shepherd; I shall not want. He makes me to lie down in green pastures; He leads me beside the still waters. He restores my soul; He leads me in the paths of righteousness for His name's sake. Yea, though I walk through the valley of the shadow of death, I will fear no evil; for You are with me; Your rod and Your staff, they comfort me. You prepare a table before me in the presence of my enemies; You anoint my head with oil; my cup runs over. Surely goodness and mercy shall follow me all the days of my life; and I will dwell in the house of the LORD forever."* [5]

God is not a monster but a loving father, who wants the best for His children, and provides adequately for those who obey Him. He gives them life and health, enriches them as He did the patriarchs, Abraham, Isaac and Jacob, and provides them with food, shelter, guidance and protection from their enemies.

When we speak of the Sabbath 'day,' we must clearly define the term 'day.'

The opening scripture defines a '*day*' as 'the evening and the morning." That phrase continues from the first day to the seventh. **"And God called the light Day, and the darkness He called Night. And there was evening and there was morning, one day."** [6]

We must therefore calculate a biblical day from the going down of the sun in the disappearance of light that lasts for twenty-four hours, one full rotation of the earth around the sun. The spiritual significance of this is that the sun is always shining twenty-four hours every day of the year. God is light, and while all things animate and inanimate move around Him, He is never in darkness, even when we are.

From this first passage, we become aware that a day also begins not as traditionally interpreted "in the morning and ends when the sun goes down," but a biblical 'day' begins the 'evening' before and ends just before the next evening. In our Greek named days, the first day of the week begins on Saturday evening and ends Sunday before darkness descends on the earth.

How many days are given 'unto man' and how many 'unto the Lord'? It is also clear that although the God of Israel owns every day, in a very special way He *separated the seventh day* from all other days *for Himself.*

We may compare this to a man who owns seven homes, but as the owner, He designates only one in which he will live. The other six he designates for his guests and his friends. It is the right of a very rich man to do as he pleases with what he owns.

Did God give specific instructions for spiritual, mental, emotional and physical rest at regular intervals every week? If He has, we would be wise to be adequately prepared.

Since God has promised more care for each of His children than for sparrows, His love has inspired Him to provide us with twenty-four hours, *one complete day of rest* and refreshment in His presence! That day He has defined in clear terms: *the Seventh day* and He has placed His supreme blessing upon it and called it **"My holy day!"** [7]

The scriptures clearly teach that God created the Sabbath to begin on the evening of the Sixth day and finish on the evening of the Seventh day.

When we lay aside the clear instructions of any commandment of the Lord, we are sowing future trouble for ourselves. When we disregard the scheduled, appointed time He has set so that we might listen and learn His ways, disaster darkens on the horizon of our lives. When we slip **the Lord's holy day** into the background of our lives, we are ensuring that God takes a back seat in our priorities, and that we will fail to spend adequate time in His presence. We then become losers, ignorant of His purposes, and begin to choose our own influences that destroy our character and our lives.

The giving of the Ten Commandments to Moses was no casual affair, but highly dramatic and of great significance. God so created it, in order to impress upon the people that God was not only holy, that is, separate, and beyond human comprehension, but that He was deeply committed to the covenant and the details of the responsibilities He expected of them. His deep desire was for them to maintain a loving relationship with Him.

Let us therefore continue our investigation until we have convincing evidence of the truth, the whole truth and nothing but the truth.

NOTES

[1] Exod 19:16-24; 20:10

[2] Gen 1:3

[3] Gen 2:1-2

[4] John 5:19

[5] Psa 23

[6] Gen 1:5

[7] Isa 58:13

14
Accept no Substitute

*S*educing spirits often gradually lead even well meaning people to believe that they can find love and abiding satisfaction in material things. However, as we will discover, for some things there can never be any substitutes.

If you were a doctor with a female patient sitting before you, you would explain the necessary medications to her. *"The Lisinopril is for the blood pressure, once daily before bedtime."*

If the patient suffered with overweight, whose arms seemed like they would burst the sleeves around them, whose belly she had strapped in with a thick leather belt, but was still hanging over, she might have shrieked her objection and frowned, *"Doctor, I don't like tiny white tablets, they remind me of little grubby insects. They give me goosebumps."*

Two nurses nearby in white uniforms may have looked at each other, but you would still say, *"I'm sorry, but there are **no** substitutes!"* You would put the prescription slip into the patient's hands.

The need for rest is so crucial to man's well-being that God has designed the right prescription: the Seventh Day Sabbath, one complete day of refreshing rest that lifts the spiritual, emotional, mental and physical man into His presence.

Unless a specific time is separated and dedicated for rest, something innate in fallen human nature drives the ordinary individual to be constantly working to achieve goals. In spite of all this, God in His loving compassion has a prescription for our human frailty and propensity to go our own way.

Each person must face the choice of living by works or by faith. To live by faith is to live by rest and to obey God and His commandments as Supreme Lord of the Universe.

Abraham demonstrated his faith when God told him to offer up his only son as a sacrifice. He trusted God when he obeyed Him and took his only son, Isaac, to sacrifice on Mount Moriah. Therefore, his faith manifested by spending time in God's presence to hear a command and then to obey Him. Thus, he proved that he loved God more than he loved his only son.

Paul, the apostle, called it *the obedience of faith.*[1]

If a man rejects God's commandments, his heart is far from Him.

Jesus quoted the prophet, Isaiah, who wrote, **"In vain (fruitlessly and without profit) do they worship Me, ordering and teaching [to be obeyed] as doctrines the commandments and precepts of men. You disregard and give up and ask to depart from you the commandment of God and cling to the tradition of men [keeping it carefully and faithfully].** [2]

Such worship is a complete waste of God's time and the time of the individual who claims to be worshipping God.

You may even hear this said, *"While driving to work, I was worshipping the Lord."* If you ask, "Are you obeying the Lord?" You may get this answer, *"I love the Lord and I obey Him!"* Nevertheless, **the Lord's holy day** has been definitely rejected and you may hear this further comment, *"It doesn't matter as long as you are worshiping the Lord!"*

What did the Master tell the Pharisees? **"You have a fine way of rejecting [thus thwarting and nullifying and doing away** with] the commandment of God in order to keep your tradition (your own human regulations)! [3]

In other words, **"You are experts at rejecting God's Word and following your own rituals and commandments!"**

Many professing believers today are not busily washing kitchen utensils as the Pharisees of Jesus' day, but they are keeping traditions, established centuries ago by their denominations, heavily influenced by the Roman church.

We must now ask ourselves, "What substitute can anyone find for the cycle of rest that God has given as an instinct in man and throughout His wonderful creation?"

NOTES

[1] Rom 1:5; 16:26

[2] Matt 15:9 (AMPC)

[3] Mark 7:9 (AMPC)

15
Father knows Best

*J*ust think, if you were a busy single parent with three children, and if there were such a place you could go to complain about what you think was the shortsightedness of the Creator. As you enter the building, you read a large sign over a door: Department of Complaints. You open the door and see a large broad-faced woman with long-dropped earrings, and an arm tattooed with skulls. She is sitting at an executive desk, flipping pages of a TV guide.

"Complaint?" she asks in a raspy bass voice without looking up.

"I've got three children," you begin huffing and puffing. *"I have to do the cooking, ironing, folding of clothes, housecleaning etc. etc. etc. ad infinitum!"*

"So?" she breathes facetiously.

"If I had two more hands," you explain. *"I could get through and have a life!"*

"I'll note your complaint," she mutters, *"but we don't offer personal choices."*

"What kind of place is this?" you complain.

"Down the corridor," she points with the purple nail of her index finger, *"You'll see a sign that says: Department of Personal Choices!*

You scamper out as quickly as you can. In no time, you stand before an old man behind a long counter, whose jaws are sunk

The VALUE of Complete REST - BOOK 1 Finding REST in a Restless Age

in, and whose eyes look like he has not slept for days.

"What's your choice?" he asks.

"I need two more hands," your words tumble out of your mouth on the heels of each other.

"Two more hands!" he exclaims.

"Yes!" you are breathing fast. *"If I had two more hands,"* you explain, *"I could get through and have a life!"*

"Wow!" With a large checkered handkerchief, he wipes his brow and says, *"That's not one of the personal choices we offer!"*

"It isn't?" you look at him incredulously.

"If you wanted to choose a different job location," he began, *"we could help you. There's a computer...*(he points to a corner in the room)...*if you were looking to change careers, we could offer advice or put you on Google...but I'm sorry, there are just some things only the Creator decides. He gave you two hands. Personal choices? Hands are not one of them!"*

Dejected, you turn without looking back at the old man. *"So that's it! Just like that!"*

Outside in the car you turn on the ignition and repeat the old man's words, *"There are just some things only the Creator decides!"*

When it comes to the time for breakfast in home, parents make those choices, not children. There are just some things not left to children.

If we are children of God, Father knows best. He chooses the time of the week in which He wants our best attention to spend time with Him and He designates that time **"My holy day!"** [1]

When we choose any day for the Lord's Day, we lay aside the commandment of God, because it is either too inconvenient, or because we have theological misunderstandings of the teaching of the Bible on the subject, caused by wrong instruction, or our own lack of research.

However, a careful study of God's Word will reveal to the honest seeker that *God has provided everything in His Word for us to live healthy, wholesome lives.*

To understand any instruction of the Lord, every committed believer relies completely on the revelation of the Sacred Scriptures in its original language, and not upon interpretations of men throughout the centuries.

Although many good things and well-intentioned suggestions or teachings may come from men, yet without a doubt, much error has been perpetuated throughout the history of the church that has wrought havoc to the pure truth of what our Lord gave to free us from bondage to the devil. Therefore, a thorough in-depth examination of passages that propound any teaching must be followed from its first reference through to its last. In addition, in every case we must take into account its context and historical background.

Jesus always rebuked the Pharisees for their ignorance of the scriptures. **"You are mistaken, not knowing the Scriptures nor the power of God."** [2]

One day after Jesus had healed a man crippled for thirty-eight years, Pharisees met Him in the temple and accused Him of healing on the Sabbath day. However, He answered, **"Most assuredly, I say** to you, the Son can do nothing of Himself, but what He sees the Father do; for whatever He does, the Son also does in like manner." [3]

Thus, He always demonstrated a submission to every one of the commandments and laws of God, because He was confident that His Father knew what was best for Him. **Jesus had no problem with the Seventh Day Sabbath and He has reinterpreted it correctly for us.**

Paul, the apostle, warns us, *"Now all these things happened to them as examples, and they were written for our admonition, upon whom the ends of the ages have come."* [4]

In the revelation that God gave to John, the apostle, Jesus Himself warned the early churches, **"He who has an ear, let him hear what the Spirit says to the churches."** [5]

God created the Sabbath for all mankind. As Creator of the universe, He alone knows what is best for His children.

NOTES

[1] Isa 58:13

[2] Matt 22:29 (paraphrase)

[3] John 5:19

[4] 1 Cor 10:11

[5] Rev 3:22

16
The Supreme Example

*A*lmighty God, Maker of Heaven and earth, in Whom all life, strength and might exist, and Who is the source of all things, demonstrated from creation how to build our lives close to Him on a foundation that will provide true rest.

He never became tired, nor suffered from stress or overwork. Since He exists outside of the circuits of night and day, He is never pressured by time constraints. He is the source and foundation of all rest, the fountain of Love, Joy and Peace. Therefore, the need for rest is not His but ours.

"Have you not known? Have you not heard? The Everlasting God, the LORD, the Creator of the ends of the earth, neither faints nor is weary. His understanding is unsearchable." [1]

This world was not created by the physical work of God. He simply said, **"Let there be light,"** and there was light. **"Let the earth bring forth grass!"** and grass appeared across the face of the earth. By His words, every material thing came into existence. The rest that He experienced came from His exercise of faith, and this complete resting in faith He calls upon each of His children to experience. This is what Jesus meant when He encouraged His disciples, **"Have the faith of God!"** [2]

The writer to the Hebrews informed us that *"The worlds [during the successive ages] were framed (fashioned, put in order, and equipped for their intended purpose) by the word of God, so that what we see was not made out of things which are visible."*

Go back to the time when God was creating the world. Hear Him speaking everything into existence.

"Let there be a firmament in the midst of the waters, and let it divide the waters from the waters. Let the waters under the heavens be gathered together into one place, and let the dry land appear.

Let there be lights in the firmament of the heavens to divide the day from the night; and let them be for signs and seasons, and for days and years; and let them be for lights in the firmament of the heavens to give light on the earth; let the waters abound with an abundance of living creatures, and let birds fly above the earth across the face of the firmament of the heavens."

Then God said, "Let the earth bring forth the living creature according to its kind: cattle and creeping thing and beast of the earth, each according to its kind."

And God blessed them, saying, "Be fruitful and multiply, and fill the waters in the seas, and let birds multiply on the earth."

Then God created man in His own image.[4] After six days of extensive work creating the heavens and the earth, God instituted the SEVENTH DAY as HIS DAY.

God, Himself, therefore set the example by showing us that it is extremely beneficial to stop working, and to rest, since our human frailty demands a time of regular refreshment. For that reason, He blessed and set apart the Seventh Day for us to spend with Him.

"On the Seventh Day God ended His work which He had done; and He rested on the seventh day from all His work which He had done. And God blessed (spoke good of) the seventh day, set it apart as His own, and hallowed it, because on it God rested from all His work which He had created and done."

Having completed all of His work, He put a special blessing

upon the Seventh Day. No other day is as blessed as the seventh day. *The Hebrew word "qadosh" translated 'hallow' means 'to separate' or 'make holy' 'to set apart for a definite divine purpose.'*

The source of all rest, therefore, finds its origin in God. God Himself is the Originator of the Sabbath. The Sabbath finds its root and foundation in Him, and as a firm foundation, properly built, it facilitates and establishes an abiding intimacy with our Creator. This relationship with the Supreme God of the universe requires quality, concentrated time.

Scripture puts the Sabbath into its right perspective.

"In six days the Lord made the heavens and the earth, the sea, and all that is in them, and rested the Seventh Day. That is why the Lord blessed the Sabbath day and hallowed it [set it apart for His purposes]" [5]

We can imagine Paul, the apostle, taking up his ancient quill as he writes to Colossian believers and makes an amazing statement implying that Jesus Christ is no mere man, nor just another great prophet, but the image of the invisible God.

He further explains the depth of that statement when he writes, *"By Him all things were created that are in heaven and that are on earth, visible and invisible, whether thrones or dominions or principalities or powers. All things were created through Him and for Him. And He is before all things, and in Him all things consist,"* which means that He is the Creator of all things including the Biblical DAY OF REST. [6]

Jesus Christ therefore instituted the Sabbath as a firm foundation upon which we can securely build our relationship with God.

We may ask, "From what does modern man seem to suffer

most?" Time to accomplish all his goals, time to spend with God.

Without that scheduled time, he will place God in the background of his life, while he runs back and forth through all the earth seeking peace and rest for his soul and finding none.

God has set a time in which we must stop and rest from all our labors and sit in His presence to learn from Him His thoughts and His ways and to know Him intimately.

God created a special day, set apart from all other days, so that following His example of faith, all men everywhere could lay aside work and striving and trust Him completely.

In all this, we can discern that God is not playing games with His people. He is very definite about what He wants from them. He wants them to forget about working so much, so that they can lay aside earthly material things, everything that will eventually turn to dust and concentrate on what really matters, on the eternal things of the spirit. Moreover, He wants their entire personalities to be deeply refreshed.

NOTES

[1] Isa 40:28

[2] Mark 11:22 (*Greek Interlinear Translation*)

[3] Heb 11:3 (AMPC)

[4] Gen 1: 24 - 26

[5] Gen 2:2, 3 (AMPC); Exod 20:11 (AMPC)

[6] Col 1:15-17

17
An Old Commandment

Since the early believers and in particular Paul, the great apostle, upheld the Law of God, we too must do the same and not hold stubbornly to unresearched data, suggesting that God no longer requires His people to obey His laws. Many maintain that after the resurrection of Christ, believers need only to love God and their fellowmen. This argument therefore paves the way to eliminate any need to obey God's laws.

Of course, such twisted reasoning does not do away with any of the Ten Commandments except the fourth, which declares, **"The Seventh Day is a Sabbath of the Lord, your God!"**

Some quote scripture that seems to suggest that loving God and neighbor is enough, so that believers may now disregard the Ten Commandments, since love summarizes the Law. They willfully forget that no summary ever discards its original document.

Jesus confidently told His disciples, **"Assuredly, I say to you, till heaven and earth pass away, one jot or one tittle will by no means pass from the law till all is fulfilled"** [1]

Whenever God is not Absolute Ruler in our lives, we rebel against the laws in His Word and against those, He has delegated to rule over us. (N.B. An examination of the surrounding verses in the above references will reveal that Jesus was speaking about the Ten Commandments).

One thing is clear; mankind has an instinctive need for law. From the beginning, God has established the entire universe on definite laws so that we may live peaceful and successful lives.

However, the devil has labored from that time to undermine every one of His laws.

Paul, the apostle, writing to Roman believers explained that "[The real function of] the Law is to make men recognize and be conscious of sin [not mere perception, but an acquaintance with sin which works toward repentance, faith, and holy character]" [2] Hence, the deep need for law and order in our lives.

For this reason, Jesus carefully reinterpreted God's Law for us.

When John, the apostle wrote, **"A new commandment I give to you, that you love one another; as I have loved you,"** [3] He was not discarding the greatest commandments in the Torah. He was bringing fresh insight into a commandment every Jew had already learned from childhood.

Finally, a glimpse of John will help us to determine if believers in this age should discard the Ten Commandments and especially God's holy day.

John had been imprisoned as a criminal for preaching the good news of Jesus Christ, the Messiah. He had refused to back down on the message that he had been preaching for years.

We see John, a Jew, who all his life had been careful to respect the Ten Commandments. He is now an old man. He knew that Israel had been punished and sent into captivity more than once for discarding God's commandments and for profaning **God's holy day**.

He is sitting with parchment before him, a quill in his hand, contemplating carefully every thought before he dips the tip of his ancient pen in ink. He scratches his beard, and confidently adds this profound concept as he writes to believers with all the sincerity and love in his heart,

"Brethren, I write no new commandment to you, but an old commandment which you have had from the beginning." [4]

Observe carefully! What year was this? Researchers declare that he wrote the first letter from prison about the year A.D. 90. Ninety years after the resurrection of Jesus Christ his faith was still steadfast.

What John was preaching he had taken from the Jewish "Tanach," what Christians today call the "Old Testament." Believers had no New Testament to guide them how to live godly lives. They had the words of Jesus in their hearts, a correct interpretation of how God wanted them to live out His commandments.

That is why Paul could write to the Romans and declare that with the advent of the Messiah, *"The righteousness of the law might be fulfilled in us."* [4]

The Amplified Bible may help us to understand the passage a little clearer: *For no person will be justified (made righteous, acquitted, and judged acceptable) in His sight by observing the works prescribed by the Law. For [the real function of] the Law is to make men recognize and be conscious of sin [not mere perception, but an acquaintance with sin which works toward repentance, faith, and holy character].*

Thus, it is possible to obey God, not by the motivation of our fleshly instincts, but only through the power of the Spirit.

Therefore, we can see how a thorough research for the truth of God's Word will help us to obey the laws of God and give Him the position He rightly deserves as Lord. In this way He can bring us into the spirit of rest He so longs to bestow upon us.

So far, we can safely conclude that God blessed **the SeventhDay** and set it apart. He called it **"MY HOLY DAY,"** so that we might become intimate with Him. Knowing Him closely would make us aware of our exceedingly sinful nature and protect us from anarchy, rebellion and confusion. He could then lead us to live peaceful and constructive lives for His glory.

Therefore, from our detailed investigation, and from all the stated reasons, we may add an important observation. **The Seventh Day**, though commanded of Israel at first, still remains as **God's holy time**. That day God has separated for us to spend quality time with our Creator, and is to be kept also by New Covenant believers in these perilous days.

In addition, when King Jesus returns to earth, all nations will go up to Jerusalem to celebrate **God's Holy Day. On that day,** they will worship Him Who sits on the throne and they will bless His holy name! [6]

NOTES

[1] Matt 5:18

[2] Rom 3:20 (AMPC)

[3] John 13:34

[4] 1 John 2:7

[5] Rom 8:4 (AMPC)

[6] Isa 66:23; Rev 5:13

Questions and Answers

THE NEED FOR REST

God is not as interested in the physical rest of His people as in their spiritual rest (Heb 3:15; 4:1-9).

Although God always places a priority on the spiritual, since the spiritual is part of a triunity (i.e. spirit, soul and body), it is not possible to separate the physical outworking of the spiritual from the soul and body of man. That is why Paul, the apostle wrote, *"May the God of peace Himself sanctify you through and through [separate you from profane things, make you pure and wholly consecrated to God]; and may your spirit and soul and body be preserved sound and complete [and found] blameless at the coming of our Lord Jesus Christ (the Messiah)"* (1 Thess 5:23 AMPC).

The passage referred to in the question relates to the Israelites when Joshua was leading them toward Canaan, the Promised Land, and is a kind of allegory. The Promised Land is the place where Israelites would not be passing through uncertain territory in an unsettled state, but a place where God had promised to give them rest from their enemies, *if they obeyed His laws.*

Canaan was later renamed Jerusalem. King David once prayed, *"Arise, O Lord, to Your resting-place, You and the ark [the symbol] of Your strength."* Moreover, He gave the reason, *"For the Lord has chosen Zion, He has desired it for His habitation: this is My resting-place forever [says the Lord]; here will I dwell, for I have desired it"* (Psa 132:8, 13, 14 AMPC).

Joshua pictures for us Jesus Christ leading His people into the victorious life. However, some who had heard that God would lead them successfully, provide and protect them along the way did not believe with their whole hearts. The result was that they lived in fear, distrusted their leaders, rebelled and wanted to return to Egypt.

The writer to the Hebrews quotes from another Psalm of David, *"Today, if you will hear His voice, harden not your hearts as at Meribah and as at Massah in the day of temptation in the wilderness, when your fathers tried My patience and tested Me, proved Me, and saw My work [of judgment].*

Forty years long was I grieved and disgusted with that generation, and I said, It is a people that do err in their hearts, and they do not approve, acknowledge, or regard My ways. Wherefore I swore in My wrath that they would not enter My rest [the land of promise]" (Psa 95:7-11 AMPC).

God was angry with them, and took an oath not to let those enter Canaan, who did not put their complete trust in Him. In fact, they all died in the wilderness, and only Joshua and Caleb from that generation entered with the children of those who perished through their unbelief (Num 14:30, 38; 26:65; 32:12).

The illustration is relevant, because many, who profess faith in Jesus Christ, when the road gets rough, turn around and return to their former life. Having a restful spirit of confidence only comes from complete trust in Jesus Christ as the Captain of our salvation.

When the Israelites reached Canaan, did God discard the Ten Commandments and in particular the Seventh Day Sabbath? We know that once they entered Jerusalem, the Sabbath became a part of their weekly observance (2 Kings 4:23).

Later, when they kept mocking the prophets, despising His words and scoffing at them, God's wrath rose against them. Then there was no remedy, and His prophets could only announce a fearful looking for judgment. God "brought against them the king of the

Chaldeans, who killed their young men with the sword in the house of their sanctuary, and had no compassion on young man or virgin, on the aged or the weak. He gave them all into his hand. All the articles from the house of God, great and small, the treasures of the house of the LORD and the treasures of the king and of his leaders, all these he took to Babylon.

Then they burned the house of God, broke down the wall of Jerusalem, burned all its palaces with fire and destroyed all its precious possessions. Those who escaped from the sword he carried away to Babylon, where they became servants to him and his sons until the rule of the kingdom of Persia, to fulfill the word of the LORD by the mouth of Jeremiah, the prophet, until the land had enjoyed her Sabbaths. As long as she lay desolate she kept Sabbath, to fulfill seventy years" (2 Chron 36:16-21).

Therefore, we know that *"entering into God's rest"* means coming into a place of faith where we trust God completely. Joshua, Caleb, and all the faithful who followed them trusted God with all their hearts. However, when they arrived in Jerusalem, the place of God's rest, God did not release them from the need to spend time with Him on the Sabbath, nor from the need to meditate in His Word, nor from the need to rest physically on the Sabbath (Joshua 1:6-8).

Finally, in the Early Church days, when Jews, vacillating and discouraged because of pressure from their relatives, were considering returning to ritualistic religion, the writer to the Hebrews appealed to them. **"Today, if you hear His voice, do not harden your hearts. God limits the opportunity to trust Him to TODAY!"** The writer encouraged Hebrews to put their trust in Israel's Messiah, and enter into the blessedness of spiritual rest.

Nothing in this passage suggests that enjoying spiritual rest through faith in Christ releases God's holy day from our calendars and from spending time with Him as He commanded.

Is not the rest of the Sabbath a symbol of our rest in Christ? (Matt 11:28)

The Bible nowhere calls or refers to the Sabbath as a symbol. God called it a sign or signpost, i.e. something pointing to something else.

God told Moses to tell the Israelites, **"It is a sign between Me and the Israelites forever; for in six days the Lord made the heavens and earth, and on the seventh day He ceased and was refreshed"** (Exod 31:17). That is, it is a sign pointing back to creation, reminding us that God, not "evolution" is the Creator of heaven and earth and all that is in them.

Observe also that even after Christ had been crucified, New Covenant believers still kept the Sabbath according to the scriptures. "The women who had come with [Jesus] from Galilee followed closely and saw the tomb and how His body was laid. Then they went back and made ready spices and ointments (perfumes). On the Sabbath day they rested in accordance with the commandment" (Luke 23:55, 56 AMPC).

In the New Covenant, Paul, the apostle, refers to marriage as an illustration of Christ's relationship to the church. This, however, does not obliterate marriage (Ephesians 5:31-32, 2 Corinthians 11:2).

Paul also wrote to the Galatian believers and told them that *"there is [now no distinction] neither Jew nor Greek, there is neither slave nor free, there is not male and female; for you are all one in Christ Jesus"* (Gal 3:28 AMPC).

This also does not obliterate the sexual differences between men and women. In coming before God for salvation, it does not matter if you are male or female. However, male and female still exist, and men must marry women.

Christ also, working for our salvation and finishing that work on the cross, does not cancel our need to work six days every week. Neither does the fact that He rested from the work of salvation cancel our need to rest on **the Lord's Day**.

However, **the Sabbath is not a symbol, but a signpost.**

Firstly, the Sabbath points back to the creation, and is a reminder that God is the Creator, not man, angels, or evolution, as some would like us to believe.

Secondly, the Sabbath is a signpost pointing to a definite goal or spiritual place where God wants to take His people.

Thirdly, the Sabbath points to a covenant that God made with Israel, and reminds us that the covenant was an eternal covenant that would never pass away. In addition, we must be careful to recognize that in the last days God began bringing believing Gentiles into this same covenant.

The mission of the Messiah, Jesus Christ, was to reconcile the entire world to His Father. That is why He said, i) **"I have glorified You on the earth. I have finished the work which You have given Me to do." ii) "I have manifested Your name to the men whom You have given Me out of the world. They were Yours, You gave them to Me, and they have kept Your word." iii) "I have given to them the words which You have given Me, and iv) "As You sent Me into the world, I also have sent them into the world."** (John 17:4, 6, 8, 18).

Fourthly, the Sabbath points to God's example of working, and emphasizes that all mankind must work. It also points to God's example of finishing the work He had begun. Believers should follow that example and not start anything without God's direction, and once directed by Him, they should finish the work He has given.

Mental health experts confirm the benefit of work to the human psyche. When human beings do not work, psychological problems arise. Many become confused, depressed, abusive and even suicidal.

God has ordained that man should work six days every week for spiritual, physical, emotional and mental health reasons. When He created the universe in six days, He, Himself, set the example of working.

Paul, the apostle, in writing to Thessalonian believers declared, *"While we were yet with you, we gave you this rule and charge: If anyone will not work, neither let him eat"* (2 Thess 3:10).

Fifthly, the Sabbath points to God's example of resting at a set time. *"On the seventh day He ceased and was refreshed"* (Exod 31:17).

Mental health experts confirm that adequate rest is essential to a vibrant mental state. Sleep experts recommend sufficient sleep each night, but deep sleep they say is related to hard work that precedes sleep.

Our Creator therefore demonstrated His wisdom when He set the example in scheduled work and scheduled rest. For that reason, He set apart the seventh day, the final day of every week for all creation to rest and be refreshed.

The Sabbath therefore is not a symbol of our rest in Christ, as many believers convince themselves. *It is a signpost*, a point in the path of life, where we find a wise direction for God to bless us. The signpost says, "Work six days every week. When you have completed the work your Father in Heaven has given you, like God, stop everything that you are doing and rest, so that you may be refreshed."

Believers ought to be resting in Christ through faith every day. Jesus was resting all the time. He said, **"the Son is able to do nothing of Himself (of His own accord); but He is able to do only what He sees the Father doing, for whatever the Father does is what the Son does in the same way [in His turn],"**

Again, he said, "I am able to do nothing from Myself [independently, of My own accord - but only as I am taught by God and as I get His orders]" (John 5:19; John 5:30 AMPC). **"What I am telling you I do not say on My own authority and of My own accord; but the Father Who lives continually in Me does the (*His*) works (His own miracles, deeds of power)"** (John 14:10 AMPC).

Jesus made it clear to His disciples that He was not the one doing the miracles and good works. He rested in spirit, and allowed the Father to work through Him.

However, Jesus still celebrated the Sabbath rest. The idea that because a believer is resting by faith in Christ all the time allows the devil to subtly rob the believer of physical, emotional and mental rest by keeping him busy seven days every week.

For that reason, we find many believers dying before their time. They subscribe to that ungodly philosophy and trick of the devil that they should be busy for God seven days every week. They disobey God's command to **remember His holy Day**, and that the **Seventh Day** belongs to the Lord and to Him alone, a day to spend with their eternal Lover.

Like the hymn writer we ought to say, "Lord Jesus Christ we seek Thy face, within the veil we bow the knee; Oh, let Thy glory fill this place, and bless us while we wait on Thee. Shut in with Thee, far, far above, the restless world that wars below etc."

What substitute is there for spending time in the presence of the King of kings and Lord of lords? You enter weary, worn and distressed, but you leave refreshed because you found joy in His presence. *"In His presence is fullness of joy, and at His right hand, there are pleasures forevermore"* (Psalm 16:11).

Of joy in His house, the Lord promised, **"All these I will bring to My holy mountain and make them joyful in My house of prayer. Their burnt offerings and their sacrifices will be accepted on My altar; for My house will be called *A HOUSE OF PRAYER for ALL peoples."*** (Isa 56:7)

Does not the scriptures teach that the SABBATH was A SHADOW of the believer's rest through faith? If so, where?

Many people have been taught and truly believe that God's rest on the seventh day (Genesis 2:3) foreshadowed a future Sabbath Rest. However, **nowhere in scripture does the Bible state that the seventh day Sabbath foreshadowed a future Sabbath.**

That subtle twist suggests that the Sabbath was a shadow that would eventually pass away. Heb 10:1 states that *the law HAD a shadow*. Yes, it did. The sacrifices and objects in the tabernacle all reflected some aspect of the coming Messiah, and were all to pass away.

Often you may hear believers misquoting this verse and saying, "The Law is a shadow." No, the Law HAD a shadow. That is a different thing!

Again, this is only another excuse for people who want to be free from the commandment to separate a regular time to rest on the seventh day. It is also a trick of the devil to keep believers working seven days every week so that he can steal, kill and destroy their lives. Today believers are not only falling into this trap but also receiving the consequences of their disobedience to the clear commandment of the Lord.

Did not the apostle Paul teach that the Sabbath was temporary and foreshadowed the New Covenant rest, which those who trust in Christ would experience?

Another argument some use against the Seventh Day Sabbath comes from Paul's letter to the Colossians, asserting that the Sabbath is mentioned only after Paul began to focus on the Gentiles and warned, *"Do not let anyone judge you by what you eat or drink, or with regard to a religious festival, a New Moon celebration or a Sabbath day. These are a shadow of the things that were to come; the reality, however, is found in Christ."* (Col 2:16 -17).

However, take note of the plural "These are." The collection of false teachings by the Gnostics is regarded as transient as a shadow cast by the sun that would soon disappear.

Paul is not saying that the Seventh Day Sabbath is a shadow. He is saying that to follow the Gnostic teaching does not bring a believer into superior knowledge and wisdom, but that the rigid observance of Gnostic rules was flimsy in comparison to the fullness into which those who trust Christ would come by following Him.

Of course, anyone wanting to escape from the seventh day Sabbath rest would be happy to use this argument in order to work seven days every week.

Does not the attempt to keep the SABBATH lead believers into

BONDAGE and therefore disturbs the believer's sense of rest?

Some quote the following verse in Galatians as a standard defense to declare that obeying God's command to observe the Sabbath brings the New Covenant believer into bondage. *"But now that you know God - or rather are known by God - how is it that you are turning back to those weak and miserable principles? Do you wish to be enslaved by them all over again? You are observing special days and months and seasons and years"* (Galatians 4:9–10).

The historical context of this passage reveals that Jewish teachers known as Judaizers, had been traveling through New Testament congregations insisting that only those who followed the Law of Moses be considered genuinely saved. Salvation not only included faith in Christ but also the strict observance of the Mosaic Law, which included circumcision. Paul was teaching that faith alone was the ONLY requirement necessary to enter the kingdom of God.

Once more, to be able to escape the Seventh Day rest that Jesus commands as Lord of the Sabbath, some quote this passage in order to allow believers to be free to work seven days every week.

Nowhere in scripture is the SABBATH given as a DAY OF WORSHIP!

This, on the surface may seem to be true. Is there anything wrong with worshipping on Saturday? Absolutely not! We should worship God every day, not just on Saturday or Sunday!

The issue of worship is not the primary concern in this research, although it is most important. The issue is one of rest. Should Christians work seven days every week? Has God set apart a time in which His people may be free from material considerations and selfish goals? Yes. The prophet Isaiah outlines the program that will save our lives and that of generations to come (Isa 58:13, 14). And Jesus Himself expected the observance of that day even after He had returned to His Father (Matt 24:20).

Moreover, when He returns to reign in Jerusalem, from one Sabbath to the next ALL FLESH (all nations) shall come to worship before God (Isa 66:23).

From the prophecy of Isaiah, it is clear that in the new Jerusalem the Sabbath will also be a day of worship for all mankind. In addition, as Jesus taught, the Ten Commandments were given with a purpose to give life and benefit to all mankind, not to be an enemy or a curse against anyone (Mark 2:27; Matt 19:17).

The Appointed Day

Can you prove that the seventh day that you keep is truly the seventh day ancient Sabbath coming down in continual succession from the day on which God rested? If not, your day is no better than any other day. And if you can, how can all men everywhere observe the same seventh day Sabbath? If you believe this, explain how a traveler going around the earth, if going east, gains one hour every thousand miles and how far would he go before losing count? Explain also how those living far away in the extreme climates of the earth can keep the Sabbath when they experience six months of night and six months of day throughout the ages.

The command to keep the Sabbath day was certainly given first to the Israelites. The Israelites were commissioned by God to be a holy nation, a priesthood to bring light to all the nations. At the same time, the light and understanding of the Sabbath was intended to bring every kind of rest needed for the human personality.

When the Jews failed to obey God, He selected twelve Jewish men, a remnant who believed, trained them for three and a half years and released them to preach the good news of rest from sin, and deliverance from every kind of bondage that would destroy the souls and bodies of men.

Those early apostles all kept the Sabbath day. The Early Church imitated them by going to the synagogue on the Sabbath days. In addition, there exists on record those throughout the centuries who have not yielded to tradition and carnal arguments not to keep God's commandments.

A quick peak at an internet website revealed very excellent answers to the above questions.

First inquiry: "So how long are the days and nights in Alaska?"

"Alaska has normal 24 hour days."

Another website provided this information:

"As artificial lighting improved, especially after the Industrial Revolution, night time activity has increased and become significant to the economy in most places. Establishments, such as nightclubs, bars, convenience stores, fast-food restaurants, distribution facilities, gas stations, and police stations now operate twenty-four hours a day or stay open as late as 1 or 2 a.m. Even without artificial light, moonlight sometimes makes it possible to travel or work outdoors at night."

Here is a comment that deals with people living in northern regions:

Rabbi Israel Lipschutz, in his commentary *Tiferet Yisrael*

writes that in polar regions a 24-hour day exists, since the sun rotates in the sky from a high point at noon to a low point near the horizon at midnight. A means of measuring the passage of a 24-hour day during the polar winter cannot be offered when the sun is invisible. However, Jewish travelers are advised to observe the beginning and end of the Sabbath based on the clock of the location from where they came. It is not clear whether this refers to residence or port of embarkation.[1]

This perspective means that two Jews who depart from different cities will always observe the Sabbath on Saturday, though at different times. A Jew departing from America would observe the Sabbath according to the clock of his hometown, while a Jew from Europe would be guided by the clock of his European hometown, which begins and ends the Sabbath about five hours earlier than in America. Therefore, the polar regions do not have any unique beginning and end of the day that may be identified.

From this information, we can deduce that none can escape the Word of God about the seventh day Sabbath. Every country worldwide has a seven-day week. In every country there is a first day of the week and a seventh day of the week. God is well aware that the earth moves around the sun. He also knows that every serious believer who loves Him can count and discover in any country which day of the week is the seventh day.

God's commandment still remains: **"the Seventh Day is a Sabbath to the Lord your God; in it you shall not do any work, you, or your son, your daughter, your manservant, your maid-servant, your domestic animals, or the sojourner within your gates"** (Exod 20:10).

"If you turn away your foot from [traveling unduly on] the Sabbath, from doing your own pleasure on My holy day, and call the Sabbath a [spiritual] delight, the holy day of the Lord,

honorable, and honor Him and it, not going your own way or seeking or finding your own pleasure or speaking with your own [idle] words, then will you delight yourself in the Lord, and I will make you to ride on the high places of the earth, and I will feed you with the heritage [promised for you] of Jacob your father; for the mouth of the Lord has spoken it (Isa 58:13, 14 AMPC).

The twenty-four hours of the Seventh Day Sabbath belong exclusively to the Lord God of the Universe. That time does not belong to any human being, race, nation or people, although the commandment was first uttered to Israelites hearing an awesome voice from heaven, and seeing a burst of fire and billowing smoke on Mount Sinai. But the Lord still says, **"I am the Lord, I do not change"** (Mal 3:6).

W as not the day when the Lord appeared especially to Thomas a day of rejoicing and gladness?

Certainly, it was wonderful that Thomas received a special visitation of the Lord in spite of his unbelief. However, the first day of the week was never the Sabbath, and never referred to in scripture as the Lord's Day, except by people who wish to substitute their tradition for the Word of God.

Thunder, lightning and a mountain bursting forth fire and billowing smoke preceded the voice of the Lord God as He proclaimed, **"The seventh day is a Sabbath to the Lord your God!"** (Exod 20:10)

Nowhere in scripture is there even a slight suggestion that the Lord God changed the Seventh Day to the first day of the week.

Let God be praised! The angels in heaven rejoice over one sinner who repents. Their rejoicing and ours can take place on any day of the week, even on the seventh day Sabbath. Jesus Christ taught that **"there is joy in the presence of the angels of God over one sinner who repents."** (Luke 15:10).

*W*as not the change from the seventh day to the first day of the week the Lord's doing, and is it not "marvelous in our eyes," as God had said? (Psa 118:23-24).

History reveals clearly that the Lord did not change the day of rest from the seventh day to the first day of the week.

Rather, it was backslidden religionists, ignorant of God's Word, who claimed that the church on earth had power to change God's laws. They even persecuted those who sought to obey God and even killed them.

Not one scripture in the entire Bible supports the view that God ever altered the word that had gone out of His lips with regard to the seventh day. The Bible clearly teaches that God had blessed and set apart the seventh day from the beginning of creation.

The seventh day was observed before Moses went up totop of Mount Sinai and received the Ten Commandments (Exod 16:22-30). The seventh day was spoken by God Himself directly to the children of Israel, who trembled exceedingly when they heard the voice of God (Exod 20:1-22).

Whatever God does is marvelous and wonderful, but changing the Sabbath day to the first day of the week was not one of them.

*W*hat day did the Lord make, if not the Lord's Day?

Amazingly, some take words out of context from a Jewish

king's psalm of praise to God and create a theology around the first day of the week.

David exhorted every faithful Jew to come into the temple of the Lord and to bring thanksgiving to Him, because of His great mercy to Israel. He was grateful that the Lord had answered his prayer and had delivered him in the time of his distress and taken him to a safe place. When surrounded by hostile men and nations, he discovered so often that trusting in God was better than trusting in ordinary men, in leaders or even those of royal birth.

He exalted the name of the Lord by which He overcame all his enemies and put them to flight. After the victory of battle, he would enter the tabernacle of the Lord to offer praise to Him, and shouts of joy would echo among those who trusted in God. This called for the sacrifice of a lamb as an offering of thanksgiving unto God. David then declared, *"This is the day that the Lord has made, we will rejoice and be glad in it!"* (Psa 118:24).

How does King David's word become translated to mean the traditional first day of the week? This seems nothing less than blind prejudice, born of ignorance of God's Word. An important consideration may even be examined. Could David have been talking about the Seventh Day Sabbath?

Isaiah, the prophet, quoted the Lord calling the Sabbath **"My holy Day."** But let us refuse to be prejudiced and consider that David may have been talking about any of the other six days of the week, for the Lord God made them all. When he returned from battle, perhaps he entered the temple immediately to give thanks to God. It is conceivable that he may have remarked that God had his hand upon that special day of victory.

However, when people want to believe something, they

will search even a haystack for a needle, and perchance when they find a stick the size of a needle, they will hold it up and claim with a loud voice, "Look! I have found a needle!"

***D**id not the Lord arise on the first day of the week? Was not that day a day of rejoicing and gladness? (Psa 118:24; Luke 24:32-41)*

In spite of what God had said through the prophet Isaiah about His holy day, to many of God's people tradition may be allowed to replace the Word of God.

Very often preachers and teachers of the Word will gather a scripture here and another there, link them together and immediately produce a new teaching.

In this case, scripture clearly tells us which day of the week is the Lord's holy day. In fact, God Himself declares that **the Seventh Day Sabbath is "My holy Day."** He even spells out the attitudes He expects of His people during the hours of that day. There can be no doubt that He is looking forward to spending time with His people, because of His great love for them (Isa 58:13).

However, with the backsliding of the Body of Christ after the death of the apostles, false teachers like wolves came in among the flock of God and brought in false teachings.

Paul, the apostle, warned young Timothy that "*in the latter times some would turn away from the faith, giving attention to deluding and seducing spirits and doctrines that demons teach*" (1 Tim 4:1 AMPC).

Paul also told the Ephesian elders before leaving them, *"I know this, that after my departure savage wolves will come in among you, not sparing the flock* (Acts 20:29).

Peter, the apostle, also warned that *"[in those days] there arose false prophets among the people, just as there will be false teachers among yourselves, who will subtly and stealthily introduce heretical doctrines (destructive heresies)"* (2 Pet 2:1 AMPC).

Perhaps the following questions will connect us to a little bit of history which might enlighten us at this time.

Did the apostles, as some claim, change the day God called "My holy day" to another day?

Acts 20:7 and 1 Cor 16:1-2 are often offered as proof that the apostles themselves discarded the Sabbath. But careful research reveals that the early believers were in fact meeting not only on the first day of the week but were so excited about the faith that they were in the temple every day and breaking bread from house to house, continually praising God and having tremendous influence on the people (Acts 2:46, 47)

Of course, everyone is aware that the early believers, both Jews and Gentiles, kept the Sabbath Day by attending services in the synagogue (Acts 14:42, 43). Luke records that the apostles expected the Gentiles to be present every Sabbath to learn from the Torah teaching in the synagogue how to serve God (Acts 15:19-21). None of the apostles ever taught that Sabbath keeping was a way to gain God's favor or to attain salvation through the forgiveness of sins.

We are assured that the apostles did not change the Seventh Day Sabbath to any other day. That much we know. It is clear from the record that they attended the synagogue and celebrated God's holy day.

On what day did the Early Church meet for worship?

Some claim that a mandate by Constantine in A.D. 321 "changed" the Sabbath from Saturday to Sunday. They also declare that the Scriptures never mention any Sabbath (Saturday) gatherings of believers for fellowship or worship. However, they insist that there are clear passages that mention the first day of the week. For example, **Acts 20:7** states that "on the first day of the week we came together to break bread."

They also quote **1 Corinthians 16:2** where Paul urged the Corinthian believers "on the first day of every week, each one of you should set aside a sum of money in keeping with his income." Since Paul designated this offering as "service" in **2 Corinthians 9:12**, this collection must have been linked with the Sunday worship service of the Christian assembly. Historically, they are convinced that Sunday,not Saturday, was the normal meeting day for Christians in the church, and its practice dates back to the first century.

However, it is clear that on the cross Christ did not cancel the Ten Commandments. However, He did cancel the code that listed judgments against those who broke the Ten Commandments. This is stated in the same passage quoted (Col 2:14) where the words "ordinances that were against us, which was contrary to us," indicate that Christ was dealing with the punishments for breaking the law, not the law itself, which Christ emphasized would never be taken away (Matt 5:17-20).

As Jesus taught, the Ten Commandments were not to be an enemy or a curse against anyone, but to give life and benefit to all mankind, (Mark 2:27; Matt 19:17).

NOTES

[1] https://en.wikipedia.org/wiki/Jewish_law_in_the_polar_regions

Conclusion

1. Christ must be loved above all else, preeminent in all things within the believer's life.

2. Throughout His creation, God has deposited the following instincts in man

   i) to rest in the Lord
   ii) to love the Lord and be loved by Him
   iii) to worship God as Creator and
   iv) to be subject to His Laws

3. God instituted **His Holy Day** at the creation of the universe.

4. God's calendar day begins in the evening at sundown from the very first day and ends at sundown on the next day.

5. To forget **the Lord's Day** destroys our relationship with Him, and thus our spiritual, emotional, mental and physical health.

6. Stubbornness opens the door for demonic deception and false teaching with regard to God's holy day and a host of other pernicious doctrines.

7. Background and family traditions can blur the truth of **the Lord's Day.**

8. The King of the Universe cordially invites all true believers to the feast of the Sabbath, a time of spiritual, emotional, mental and physical refreshing in His presence. No excuse will be accepted for being absent from the Lord's Sabbath. The invitation was formerly written on stone tablets for several thousand years and reads, "[Earnestly] remember the Sabbath day, to keep it holy (withdrawn from common employment and dedicated to God).

Six days you shall labor and do all your work, but the seventh day is a Sabbath to the Lord your God; in it you shall not do any work, you, or your son, your daughter, your manservant, your maidservant, your domestic animals or the sojourner within your gates" (Exod 20:8-10 AMP).

9. Since the establishment of the New Covenant with Israel and Judah, the law is now written in believers' hearts. (Jer 31:31-33; 2 Cor 3:3).

10. Both Jews and Gentiles who believe in Christ have become ONE IN HIM, and loving Him will obey His commandments. And His commandments are not new, no longer on stone tablets, but in the heart of every true child of God (1 John 2:7, 8).

About the Author

*R*ichard McCaw began to write at the age of ten, and his first two poems soon appeared in "The Children's Own," a weekly Jamaican children's newspaper.

Converted at the age of thirteen, he soon began to diligently study the scriptures.

At the age of fourteen, he won his school's music scholarship and later became a distinction candidate in the Royal Schools of Music yearly examinations. At the age of fifteen he began teaching a Sunday School class of ten to twelve-year-olds and soon preached his first sermon in a small country church.

As a young adult he became an associate missionary with Christian Literature Crusade, where two books in the bookstore: "A Passion for Souls" by Oswald J. Smith and "The Soul Winner's Fire" by John R. Rice inspired him to become a personal evangelist wherever he went.

Later, he became an accompanist in the voice department at the Jamaica School of Music and a violinist in two Jamaican orchestras. Then he went on to earn his licentiate (L.R.S.M.) from the Royal Schools of Music (London) and his licentiate (L.T.C.L.) from the Trinity College (London). In 1994, the Institute of Jamaica recognized him as one of Jamaica's four best music teachers.

In the mid-90's he conducted workshops in piano, guitar, violin, vocal technique in several churches and has taught Music, Spanish, Drama, Computer and Art in private schools in Fort Lauderdale, Florida. For several years he was also Senior Piano and Drama teacher for Boys' and Girls' clubs in Broward County.

Since 1965 his gifts of writing and music supported him as he ministered widely in schools, universities and churches in his homeland. Under the ministry of the Inter-Schools-Christian Fellowship and Scripture Union, an affiliate of the International Fellowship of Evangelical Students, he served as a sponsor for three prominent schools in Jamaica. He has also served as a counselor during fifteen years of ministry at Moorlands Camps in Spur Tree, Mandeville, Jamaica.

As a young adult he published eleven short stories for children, eight for teenagers, and one for adults. His novel "A Way of Escape" was serialized in "Impact for Youth," a monthly magazine that reached out to teenagers with the gospel. Two of his short stories later won him a writer's scholarship to represent Jamaica at the Caribbean Writers' and Artists' Workshop in Trinidad. His weekly devotional column for a local political newspaper reached as far as Nigeria and in the 1980's his poetry also appeared in editions of the American Poetry Anthology.

He was ordained to the ministry in 1976 and then became an elder in Covenant Community Church and the pastor of Windward Road Covenant Community Church in Kingston, Jamaica. From 1989 until 1994, he was the school pastor and guidance counselor for Covenant Christian Academy.

He also ministered in seminars and conferences in Trinidad, Monserrat, Barbados, Curacao, Cuba, Guyana, Canada, England and the United States.

Since 2013 he has been writing for a quarterly online magazine "thesharemagazine.com" that is published in London. His vision has always been to see God's people thoroughly equipped for the work of the ministry.

Made in the USA
Lexington, KY
05 February 2019